HOLLYWOOD SAID NO!

Orphaned Film Scripts, Bastard Scenes,
and Abandoned Darlings
from the Creators of *Mr. Show*

BOB ODENKIRK & DAVID CROSS

with Brian Posehn

GRAND CENTRAL
PUBLISHING

NEW YORK   BOSTON

The events and characters in this book are fictitious. Certain real locations and public figures are mentioned, but all other characters and events described in the book are totally imaginary.

Copyright © 2013 by Liberal Jew-Run Media Productions, Inc. and Le Foole, Inc.
Illustrations copyright © 2013 by Mike Mitchell
All rights reserved. In accordance with the U.S. Copyright Act of 1976, the scanning, uploading, and electronic sharing of any part of this book without the permission of the publisher is unlawful piracy and theft of the author's intellectual property. If you would like to use material from the book (other than for review purposes), prior written permission must be obtained by contacting the publisher at permissions@hbgusa.com. Thank you for your support of the author's rights.

Grand Central Publishing
Hachette Book Group
237 Park Avenue
New York, NY 10017

www.HachetteBookGroup.com

Printed in the United States of America

RRD-C

First Edition: September 2013
10 9 8 7 6 5 4 3 2

Grand Central Publishing is a division of Hachette Book Group, Inc.
The Grand Central Publishing name and logo is a trademark of Hachette Book Group, Inc.

The Hachette Speakers Bureau provides a wide range of authors for speaking events. To find out more, go to www.hachettespeakersbureau.com or call (866) 376-6591.

The publisher is not responsible for websites (or their content) that are not owned by the publisher.

ISBN 978-1-4555-2630-7
Library of Congress Control Number 2013939087

Bob and David would like to dedicate this book to the cast of Mr. Show . . . our friends, talented people, and gravely underused by Hollywood: Jay Johnston, Paul F. Tompkins, John Ennis, Brian Posehn, Jill Talley, Tom Kenny, Brett Paesel, Mary Lynn Rajskub, Jerry Minor, Scott Aukerman, B.J. Porter, and Karen Kilgariff. To Troy Miller for shining our shit to a sparkle and Eban Schletter for making us sound golden. To Mike De Luca for believing in us. To New Line for not believing in us. But mostly and sincerely to our fans—you guys have impeccable taste! And to our little man in Congress, Louie Gohmert . . . Go Big L!

Contents

Preface

Hey everybody, it's Bob and David! Before we begin we would like to go to the ol' future and answer our most-asked question about this lil' book from the ol' mailbag.

> *Dear Bob and David,*
>
> *So…what…you think if you publish your stupid screenplays that somebody in Hollyweird will actually read 'em and go, "Oh my God, we screwed up so bad, we didn't make these genius screenplays?!! We'd better fix this right away and apologize to these guys and make all their badly plotted, half-assed comedy screenplays before they, uh… what? Get us in trouble with the comedy police?!" I mean, I read your screenplays, and yeah, there were some laughs in there, but they were also kinda sloppy and waaaayy too satirical. Nobody likes satire that much, figure it out already. Anyway, I'm a fan of SOME of your work, I've written a few screenplays myself, but you don't see me trying to publish them and cutting down the last remaining trees so I can have a pity party in public. Anyway…good luck, I guess…and hey, if you'd read one of my screenplays I'd appreciate it. I got one that's about these two guys named Dob and Bavid who catch a chupacabra and train it, it's kind of an updated, cinema verité* How To Train Your Dragon.*
>
>

Seriously,
George Szondorski

> **It doesn't have to be cinema verité, it can be mockumentary or animation, or it could be a TV show…or anything.*

Thanks for your letter from the future, George, and now here's our answer: No, we don't think Hollywood people will read this book and think they made a mistake. We'll get to that in the Introduction. We are publishing these scripts because we, like you, are fans of "SOME" of our work. Where we disagree with you is in your dismissive reference to us cutting down trees. The trees have been man's worst enemy on Earth since the dawn of creation. Guess who killed the dinosaurs? The trees did. It's them or us and this is one small step in the right direction. Also, YES, we will read your screenplay! This sounds wonderful! Two guys who train a legendary mystical creature from south of the border! It's got international sales written all over it in green ink! If it's not a problem, we would like to make it an animated mockumentary for the web only! Send it ASAP—this is gonna go good!

Now, to everyone else, welcome to the book of screenplays that never got made. We hope you get some laughs out of it.

Introduction: A Brief History and Context of the Scripts Herein

Ah, Hollywood, you giveth and you taketh away, like a colicky two-year old being fed oysters. One never knows what gems or turds will manage to squirt through Hollywood's labyrinthine system and get made, their filmic fate then to be decided upon by an even more fickle populace. Will it be *Animal House*? Or will it be *Bio-Dome*? One can never be certain. We got to make a movie once. But more on that later. For, you see…

You hold in your hands a couple of movie scripts (and then some) that we wrote in reasonable anticipation of being able to get them made. Meaning these scripts were written after ending the run of *Mr. Show with Bob and David*. And with that small, yet real, measure of success in mind, the obvious next step for our rag-tag group was to write and make a movie. And of course! Why wouldn't we? *Corky Romano*? *Beverly Hills Ninja*? *Snowboard Academy*? *Joe Dirt*? With these and several others as examples of the then-current crop of comedies getting made, why wouldn't we believe a *Mr. Show* movie could do the box-office business that the aforementioned movies would do? And, hopefully, the business would be just enough to allow us to then make more films.

Well we, along with fellow *Mr. Show* writer/performers Scott Aukerman, B.J. Porter, and Brian Posehn did write that movie, and Troy Miller, our director/producer extraordinaire at *Mr. Show*, directed and edited it. It was called *Run Ronnie Run*, and unfortunately, it wasn't very good. But enough virtual ink has been spilled on that sorry saga, and if you bought this book, it's probably safe to assume you know the tortured history of it already and don't need to hear our rehashed whining again, again.

But it does provide context for this book. And helps answer the rhetorical question, why exactly are we putting out a book of film scripts that never got made?

Well, because we think they're funny and that you will enjoy reading them.

The first one we wrote (chronologically) is *Hooray for America!* (although it's not the first script you'll find in this book). *Hooray!* is a more high-concept story than we had explored on *Mr. Show* but the kind of thing we may have progressed toward if there were to have been a fifth season.* It's a linear story where we (and the *Mr. Show* cast) would play multiple roles, and several different tones of comedy are represented. But we decided that perhaps it was *too* high-concept to be our first movie, so we went back to the drawing board. That was where *Run Ronnie Run* came in, and, well, we all know how that turned out. But we were determined to make a movie, so it was back, once again, to the drawing board. This time we decided to give America what it really needed—a great sketch movie. This was *Bob and David Make a Movie*. It is the first script you will encounter in this book.

We were convinced we might actually be able to persuade someone in Hollywood (anyone!) to finance this script and get it made. In other words: cheap, not particularly challenging, and unarguably funny. We didn't know that we had reached our nadir already.

Bob and David Make a Movie starts immediately with us talking to each other and to camera. It feels very familiar to the first few minutes of *Mr. Show*: we greet the audience and each other, a situation presents itself, it then quickly spins into something else entirely, then leads us into our first sketch, and ultimately winds back around to a satisfying ending that recalls the beginning. Much simpler than *Hooray!*, more "Bob and Davidy" than *Run Ronnie Run*, and much, much more like *Mr. Show*—the lady that brought us to the dance in the first place, as it were. And the fact that we and our cast again would play multiple roles in that story as well was always exciting for us.

Needless to say, *Hooray for America!* and *Bob and David Make a Movie* were never made. And never will be. They were written for two exciting, up-and-coming comedy writer/actors in their late thirties who were coming off of a still-relevant cult comedy show to make. That ship has not only

---

*Pure conjecture on our part, but we can easily see it.

sailed but has been dry-docked and turned into a museum. But know that there is no bitterness here; we are happy in our lives and professions. Often things don't work out like one would hope (*Let's Go to Prison*, *Freak Show*) and sometimes they do (*Breaking Bad*, *Arrested Development*)—that's life. But we decided that rather than have all of this stuff languish on a couple of bookshelves in Brooklyn and L.A., we'd release it into the wild, complete with reminiscences, illustrations, and extra jokey-jokes for you to enjoy.

See you in 2015!
Bob and David

BOB AND DAVID MAKE A MOVIE

by Bob Odenkirk, David Cross,
and Brian Posehn

First draft on August 4th, 2003

ANIMATED WARNINGS

MUSIC: Upbeat fanfare throughout

NOTE: This opening piece is animated with cheap computer graphics (circa: the DIRE STRAITS video "Money For Nothing") which correspond to the announcement. In addition, it should be scratchy, with skips, like it's been shown for years—

WE SEE: Klieg lights waving madly, pull in to . . .

GIANT THEATRE MARQUEE with the title: "TONIGHT'S FEATURE-LENGTH MOVING PICTURE!"

> ANNOUNCER (V.O.)
> Congratulations, you're attending our feature film presentation! This theatre has been voted the most polite theatre in America for five years running! Please adhere to our strict standards of conduct for everyone's enjoyment! Remember, no talking or chitchat during the film. Please turn off all beepers for the duration of the movie! When enjoying refreshments, chew with your mouth closed and daub your lips with freshly laundered kerchiefs! Gentlemen, bow when a lady passes. Ladies, curtsy when a man passes . . . gas. Please refrain from soiling our bathrooms with your waste. Bathrooms are open for viewing five minutes before the movie, and five minutes after. When leaving the theatre please head straight home, do not stop to talk to strangers, friends, or family. Upon arriving home, lock and bolt your door. Sever all telephone lines, and board windows. Kill your spouse and leave their brains out on the front porch for the zombies to eat. Then, kneel beside your bed and pray to me, and I'll come to you in the night to tell you how to live. Now, sit back, and enjoy this feature-length moving picture presentation! Light up those cigarettes and start talkiiiiinnng nowww!!!

DIP TO BLACK

MUSIC: Tense suspense theme, building

OPEN ON: EXT. HOLLYWOOD BLVD

Shot with hi-def, handheld, VIDEO. We are in a small group of looky-loo
TOURISTS watching a scene from a movie being shot.

There is a camera crane above the scene of a spaceship which has crashed
and is giving off smoke. A small mob of NERDY-LOOKING GUYS mill about. The
DIRECTOR, sitting in a set chair with the name "Famous Mortimer," starts
the scene.

> DIRECTOR
> Okay, everybody in place? Okay, let's make this really
> intense. And...action!

The NERD MOB wave sticks, scream, and attack some unseen VICTIMS.

> NERDS
> Kill 'em! Get 'em!

The crane rises over this mob scene, and when it gets to its maximum
height, the Director steps up.

> DIRECTOR
> Cut! Print! That was great! We got it!

The crew applauds. The tourists disperse...we pick out Bob and David
from the tourist crowd and lead them as they walk down Hollywood
Boulevard.

> BOB
> Wow, David, huh?

> DAVID
> Yeah, Bob, movie magic!

> BOB
> (looking around)
> Where?

> DAVID
> Right there, what we just saw.

> BOB
> Oh. Yeah.

Bob talks to camera.

>   BOB (CONT'D)
>   Hello, I'm Bob.

>   DAVID
>   Oh, hi, I'm David.

>   BOB
>   We're here in Hollywood, California, to make a movie.
>   You might recognize us from your TV set.

Bob waves to a TOURIST and his WIFE.

ANGLE ON: Tourist

>   TOURIST
>   Keep it movin' honey, a pansy just hit on me.

>   DAVID
>   Anyway we're both very excited to make a movie for you.
>   Hey man, what's our movie about?

>   BOB
>   That'll take care of itself. First thing we need is
>   money. Let's start thinking about product placement.

A TEENAGER on a skateboard screeches to halt in front of Bob and David.

                      BOB AND DAVID
      Whoa!

                      DAVID
      What's up, kiddo?

                      TEENAGER
        (into camera)
      You guys are cool, but the coolest thing on two wheels
      is the new Flo-Tex tampon.

He holds up a brightly labeled box.

                      BOB
      Aren't tampons for women?

                      TEENAGER
      That's what you think, old man! I've got that fresh, easy
      feeling right now.

                      DAVID
      Wow! I want that, too!

                      TEENAGER
      You'll have to skate me for it!

He skates away, and a jingle plays.

                      JINGLE SINGER (V.O.)
      Flo-tex for meeeeennn...

      Freshness for aaaaalllll....

Flo-Tex tampons fall from the sky on happy Bob and David.

ANGLE ON: Abe Lincoln

                      ABE LINCOLN
      Ask not what a tampon can do for you...but what Flo-tex
      can do for a tampon!

ANGLE ON: David

                    DAVID
          Now in apricot!

MUSIC: Commercial Theme ends

Resume Bob and David on the street, natural sounds, handheld
look, etc.

                    BOB
          So how much did we make for that?

                    DAVID
               (putting wad of bills in pocket)
          We're set, we got our dough.

                    BOB
          Great. So let's make the movie!

ANGLE ON: David, he is standing in front of a poster for a dumb movie
called *Stupid and Stinky-er* which features two retarded characters (Bob
and David), teeth blocked out, one smelling the other's fart and smiling.
David rants in front of this image.

                    DAVID
          Bob, they don't just let you "make" a movie. You
          can't just go out there with no original idea, nothing
          to say, and no talent to not say it with and make a
          movie.

                    BOB
          Of course not, David, I never—

                    DAVID
          You have to fill out a form first.

                    BOB
          Oh.

                    DAVID
          Come on . . .

They turn and enter a nondescript DMV-type building.

BOB AND DAVID APPLY FOR MOVIE

SIGN: "Hollywood Town Hall"

INT. CITY OFFICE

MUSIC: Muzak, atmosphere

Bob and David enter and look around. The place is crowded like a DMV. Various HOLLYWOOD TYPES wait in line. A JANITOR notices them all disoriented.

> JANITOR
> (by rote)
> If you got a comedy follow the blue line, if it's a drama, yellow line, documentary is out back behind the Dumpster.

The three windows are marked: Drama, Comedy, Indie.

> BOB
> Blue line.

ANGLE ON: The COMEDY window. CARLOTTA, a black lady clerk, is listening to Kevin Smith, and thoughtlessly leafing through his latest script.

> CARLOTTA
> Okay Mr. Kevin Smith, good to see you again.

> KEVIN
> Thanks. I can't wait to make another film.

> CARLOTTA
> Okay. Do you have any stars in it?

> KEVIN SMITH
> I'm trying to get Shannon Elizabeth.

> CARLOTTA
> So...I'll put that down as a "no." How about special effects?

> KEVIN SMITH
> No, no, it's total low-budget.

> CARLOTTA
>
> Mm-hm. I don't know...has it got farts in it?

> KEVIN
>
> Well, it's sort of a "farce," I guess...

> CARLOTTA
>
> No, "farts." T-S.

> KEVIN SMITH
> (very positive)
> Oh, yeah! Big fart sequence.

> CARLOTTA
>
> You got it, honey. Here's your slip. Get your essentials
> and I'll stamp it for ya.

She hands him a slip and he exits, happily. JAMIE KENNEDY steps up to the window.

> CARLOTTA (CONT'D)
>
> Jamie Kennedy, what have you cooked up for me this
> time?

> JAMIE
> (excited)
> Okay, my movie is called *Invisible Dude*, about a guy who
> turns invisible when he gets nervous.

She doesn't respond.

> JAMIE (CONT'D)
>
> And...he likes this girl, has to conquer his problem,
> but then on his wedding day right before he's about to
> get married, his fiancée tells him her parents hate...
> invisible people.

Carlotta tries to hold back laughter, but busts up.

> CARLOTTA
>
> Jamie Kennedy, you did it again! Hilarious! And pointed!
> Very well done!

                    JAMIE
          Thank you.

She hands him a blue slip.

                    CARLOTTA
          Here's your blue slip, go fill it out, get your things,
          and come back and I'll stamp it. Next!

Bob and David step up to her window.

                    CARLOTTA (CONT'D)
          Who are you and what's your movie?

                    BOB
          We're Bob and David. We want to make a funny movie.

                    CARLOTTA
          What's it about?

                    DAVID
          All kinds of stuff. Just the funniest stuff we got.

                    BOB
          Just funny, y'know?

                    CARLOTTA
          You got any stars attached?

                    BOB
          Uhh...no, just us.

She laughs.

                    DAVID
          So if you'll just give us one of those slips, then we'll
          get on our way.

                    CARLOTTA
          No. Not today. Now if you'll excuse me, I'm on break.

She puts a sign reading "I'm on (cartoon of a guy with a bloody broken
leg)" and walks away toward the break room.

                        BOB
Dammit.

                        DAVID
All right, well, let's go drinkin'.

                        BOB
                   (angry)
No, David! Look, do you want to go back to shining
camels' asses at the racetrack?

                                                        CUT TO:

EXT. RACE TRACK, STABLES

A horse with a warming blanket over him stands in a stable behind TRAINER
wearing a fedora, suit. As the Trainer talks to camera, Bob and David
walk by in the background, covered in slop, carrying buckets ("Tekmans
Camel Shine") and rags.

GRAPHIC: "Jim Whitten, Trainer, RoseThorn Horse Track"

                        TRAINER
The horses like to have a companion, a goat, a dog,
keep 'em company. That's why we got Chip the camel over
there.

                        INTERVIEWER
Yes, but why do you have those guys shine her behind?

                        TRAINER
Hm?

The Trainer turns to see Bob and David.

                        TRAINER (CONT'D)
Hey! Hey you two, get the hell outta here!

The Trainer chases Bob and David.

                                                    CUT BACK TO:

INT. DMV TYPE ROOM—PRESENT

David, having this memory.

                    DAVID
          Well yeah, eventually.

                    BOB
          That's what I'm talking about. But we gotta prove
          ourselves first. Now we're getting that slip and we're
          making our movie.

They both look to the "break room" in back.

INT. BREAK ROOM

A sad, shitty institutional break room; Formica table, folding chairs,
wrappers littered about. Carlotta is by the vending machine, punching
buttons.

Bob and David enter.

                    BOB
          Give us one of those slips that you gave those other
          guys. Now.

                    CARLOTTA
          Excuse me? This is the break room. Employees only.

She puts some more coins in and carefully selects her item. David wants to
go, but Bob won't budge.

                    BOB
          Dammit, you...give us that slip.

                    CARLOTTA
          Don't you threaten me! Damn...

She is preoccupied with the vending machine, pressing and re-pressing the
same buttons. Finally we hear her item fall and get lodged in the machine
exit chute.

                    CARLOTTA (CONT'D)
          Oh...geez.

She hits the machine.

                    CARLOTTA (CONT'D)

> Come on, cookie, drop for Momma . . .

ANGLE ON: Digital readout: 28 seconds . . .

> VENDING MACHINE VOICE
> (British feminine voice)
> You have twenty-eight seconds before the vending chute
> is closed . . .

(STARTING RIGHT HERE we go to LETTERBOX "ANAMORPHIC" framing)

ANGLE ON: DAVID

MUSIC: Scored, suspense

> DAVID
> Are you having trouble with your cookie?

ANGLE ON: the trapped cookie, an "AUNT GRANDMA'S CHOCOLATEY DOUBLE CHIP DELITE" hanging in the chute.

ANGLE ON: Carlotta, beads of sweat on her brow. Reaching up the chute in vain.

> CARLOTTA
> It's my favorite cookie...the last one...
> (tears come to her eyes)
> My wrists...too big-boned...

> VENDING MACHINE VOICE
> T-minus twenty seconds to chute closure.

> CARLOTTA
> Oh, Jesus and St. Lucifer come to my aid in this time of great need...

ANGLE ON: Her fat wrist in the vending tunnel. She will never reach the cookie. Suddenly, appearing beside her wrist is a white-skinned, thin wrist.

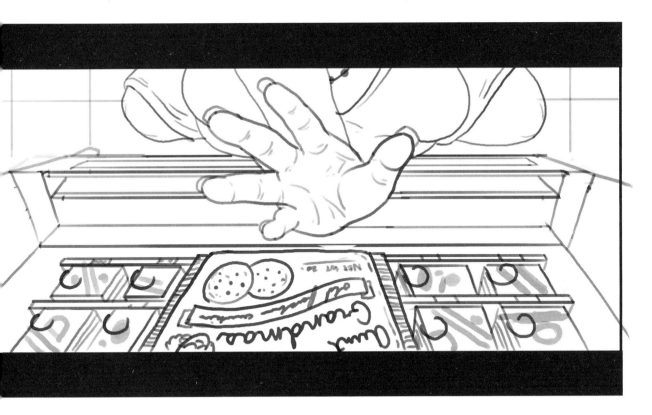

David has knelt down beside her and is reaching for the cookie.

                    DAVID
          Excuse me, ma'am, let me try.

                    VENDING MACHINE VOICE
          T-minus fifteen seconds to chute closure.

David reaches for the cookie, and...he has it!

Carlotta breathes a sigh of relief.

                    CARLOTTA
          Oh, thank you...why you have the magic hands of a
          little white girl; or a gay.

David holds the cookie in its place in the chute.

                    DAVID
          Give us one of those slips and you get your cookie.

Carlotta can't believe his audacity, holding her cookie hostage!

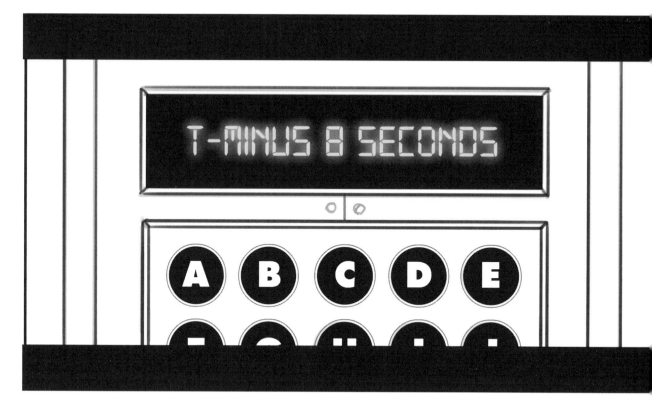

                    VENDING MACHINE VOICE
          Eight seconds to closure. seven—six—five . . .

Countdown continues through the remainder—

                         CARLOTTA
          But, I just, it's my break, I . . .

David releases the cookie, but holds his hand there, ready to grab it
again. Cornered, Carlotta pulls out a blue slip and hands it to Bob. David
snatches the cookie, and yanks his arm out of the machine, and we see a
metallic multilayered shield that could rip your arm off, snap shut.

David hands her the cookie. She begins eating greedily. Bob and David
celebrate.

                         BOB
          Awesome!

                         DAVID
          We got it!

(DROP ANAMORPHIC FRAMING)

MUSIC: Suspense scoring ends.

> CARLOTTA (O.C.)
> Well, that ain't all you need, honey.

> DAVID
> What?

Carlotta slowly eats her cookie and coyly teases the guys—she has the upper hand.

> CARLOTTA
> The blue slip is worthless without it gets stamped.

She holds up a stamp. The room darkens, except a ray of light which hits her hand holding the stamp.

Music: Ominous, *Lord of the Rings*-ey

> CARLOTTA (CONT'D)
> You just like everybody else. You need to get a few
> things first.

> DAVID
> What things?

> CARLOTTA
> First thing—you need to get your physicals. Got to be in
> tip-top shape for moviemaking! Next you need a concept,
> an idea, fish outta water or maybe just rip off ol' Harry
> Potter. Then you need you a star to shine so bright, and
> give your film an opening night. A lock of hair from a
> Producer, some famous grease from a Hollywood shmoozer.
> Lastly, approval from the Mayor of Hollywood, you get
> that, baby, and you got it good.

> DAVID
> The Mayor of Hollywood?!

Carlotta points to an oil painting of a grizzled old dude smoking a cigar, THE MAYOR OF HOLLYWOOD.

> CARLOTTA
> You have until five p.m. tonight, after that, the effects
> of this cookie wear off and I forget all about you.

She finishes the cookie and gives a self-satisfied chuckle.

                    CARLOTTA (CONT'D)
           Thanks for the cookie, cookie.

She exits.

                    DAVID
              (looking at watch)
           Shit, Bob, it's already noon. We've got a lot to do.

RINGLORD OF THE STARS

Bob and David are walking down Hollywood Blvd.

                    DAVID
           I've always dreamed of making a movie so I could see
           what all the fuss is about.

                    BOB
           What do you mean "all the fuss" . . . you've seen movies,
           right?

                    DAVID
           Does porno count?

Bob shakes his head "No." Then David shakes his head "no." Then Bob shakes his head "no" again.

                    BOB
          Let's go...

They head off, past a KOREAN STREET VENDOR with a foldout table loaded with videocassettes and DVDs.

                KOREAN STREET VENDOR
          Number one films! All films! Originals! Cheap!

A PEDESTRIAN stops by the table and peruses.

                    PEDESTRIAN
          What have you got here?

                KOREAN STREET VENDOR
          I got all number one films. Originals. You buy them.
          Be first to own. DVD or video, I don't care, you buy
          whichever, I don't care.

                    PEDESTRIAN
          Let's see...
              (reading the names)
          Star Battles, *Star Battles 2: The Return of Yodi*, *The
          Lord of DeepRing*, *SpiderFriend*...I don't know, man,
          something's fishy here.

                KOREAN STREET VENDOR
          No! No fish! DVDs, videos! You buy, take home, watch,
          laugh, cry, rethink life, maybe make different choices
          in future—

                    PEDESTRIAN
          No, these are all cheap knockoffs.

                KOREAN STREET VENDOR
          No! All originals!

A DISGRUNTLED CUSTOMER steps up, waving a videotape.

                DISGRUNTLED CUSTOMER
          Hey man, you ripped me off.

                        KOREAN STREET VENDOR
What?

                        DISGRUNTLED CUSTOMER
This is not the original.

                        KOREAN STREET VENDOR
What you buy?

                        DISGRUNTLED CUSTOMER
The Ringlord and the Star Warrior II. Uh—I wasn't paying
attention, and I'm not very smart, so I was tricked by
you.

                        KOREAN STREET VENDOR
No—it is original! You look, I show you! No returns! Top
quality!

The vendor pops the tape into a crappy monitor with a VHS machine propped
up on milk crates behind him. He presses Play and we go FULL SCREEN with
the crap title sequence to *The Ringlord and the Star Warrior II*.

(NOTE: The following "film" is shot on film, then projected in a real
theatre, and reshot with handheld video.)

GRAPHIC: The title, cut off at both sides, too big for the screen.

MUSIC: Grandiose, orchestral...but also, clearly done by one guy on his
synthesizer...in a basement in Beijing

The scenes we are about to see are all dubbed in Korean, but we will
write them and shoot them in English, because...you'll see.

OPEN ON: Establishing shots—

EXT. A FOREST

EXT. A MOUNTAINSIDE

EXT. A CUTE HUT

What I am writing are all shitty English subtitles...because we are
hearing it in Korean, remember?

> FEMALE NARRATOR (V.O.)
> One time there was a ring. This ring was mad if you were
> mad. And nice if you were nice. So, no mad person should
> ever wear it on their finger-hand.

We hear the singing voices of little people.

Camera passes through a bush to reveal a group of guys in elf costumes,
all on their knees, in a circle, singing. The audio track clicks, jumps,
and is horrible.

> ELVES
> All is well in Glooby-town, life is fun when you're a
> Glooby. We will sing and dance all day, and drink muffet
> tea by the robot friend.

They continue singing and reveal ARTIE-BLEEP-BLOOP, a squarish R2-D2
robot which is clearly a midget in a trash can, dancing around and
blooping and bleeping. (His face is cut out in a clumsy, amateur
effect.)

> ROBOT
> I love you all. I am your robot friend. We are friends
> forever. True love always. Look out, evil is all around.

EXT. RIDGE

Rising over the ridge comes our film's cheapo Darth Vader: "DEATH RAIDER"
with a flowing robe (it's Paul Tompkins on Jay Johnston's shoulders, with
a batting helmet, and an intercom taped to his mouth, and ski goggles). He
wears a paper plate with macaroni painted black as a chest plate.

Behind him comes our Gollum: "MOLLUG." This is TOM KENNY, or BLAINE
CAPATCH, wearing a dirty bodysuit, rolling a yo-yo up and down, and
slobbering.

> MOLLUG
> What do you see, Master?

> DEATH RAIDER
> We must vanquish the Gloobies! Before they bring joy to
> the universe, by being nice and wearing the ring!

Both laugh. Death Raider pulls out a "light saber," which is a flashlight, with the "saber" part scratched into the film.

                    FEMALE NARRATOR (V.O.)
          Meanwhile, somewhere else . . .

EXT. SUBURBAN HOME

Placid setting.

INT. BEDROOM

A boy named ELI is looking at something curiously. He offers, towards camera, a popsicle.

                         ELI
          Come on . . . try the happy pop! You'll like it.

ANGLE ON: A handpuppet. Or a doll held by a guy wearing all black, as though you won't see him. It shakes around and makes weird whiny noises, or the same noises as the Artie-Bleep-Bloop.

ELI (CONT'D)
What's wrong? Don't be afraid. I come in peace.

The puppet eats the popsicle.

ELI (CONT'D)
I am lost here on your planet. Just for a short time.
Can I stay in your nice suburban home?

A noise offscreen.

MOM
Honey, are you doing your homework?

Eli is scared and hides. The puppet waggles out from the closet and looks
over to the door.

A puppet mom enters through the door.

MOM (CONT'D)
I heard noises. Are you okay?

CUT BACK TO:

EXT. STREET

The Korean Street Vendor and the Disgruntled Customer have been watching
this and resume their argument. Some PASSERSBY stop to listen in.

DISGRUNTLED CUSTOMER
That's a bunch of crap! It's not what I paid for!

KOREAN STREET VENDOR
This is classic movie! Original! Changed people's lives!
No refunds! Original film!

PEDESTRIAN
Can't you tell? It's just a cheap Korean rip-off!

DISGRUNTLED CUSTOMER
No, it's not, that's the problem! I wish it was! I wanted
to purchase a cheap Korean knockoff of an American
film.

<pre>
                    PEDESTRIAN
          Why?

                DISGRUNTLED CUSTOMER
          For laughs—so I could feel my culture was superior—I
          don't know! But this thing...it's a fraud.

                KOREAN STREET VENDOR
          No, I taped it myself in shitty theatre in Korea!

                DISGRUNTLED CUSTOMER
          Then you got ripped off, man! Because this movie is a
          crappy American version of a cheap Korean rip-off of
          some overrated American classic that's been dubbed into
          Korean and then subtitled back into English!
</pre>

Everyone is a little confused.

<pre>
              DISGRUNTLED CUSTOMER (CONT'D)
          Just press Play, watch a little longer...
</pre>

Now everyone is intrigued and they start the tape again, to see the Death Raider character slaying Gloobies with his etched-in light saber. He finishes, the music is triumphant!

<pre>
                   DEATH RAIDER
          And now, Mollug, have you found the ring?
</pre>

Mollug leans into a Glooby's dying face.

<pre>
                     MOLLUG
          Where is the ring? The one true ring?

                   DYING GLOOBY
          I cannot tell you. You must ask the fairy.

                   DEATH RAIDER
          Fairy? I cannot even see fairies! I am too huge! They
          are so small!
</pre>

He laughs. The Korean dubbing cuts off, and we hear them speaking English, with terrible acting through the remainder of this piece...

                    DYING GLOOBY
          Then use this magical lens of magnification.

The Glooby holds out a magnifying glass and then dies. Mollug, the Gollum,
hands the glass to Death Raider.

                    DEATH RAIDER
          But how will I find a fairy?

                    MOLLUG
          You can hear them sing. Listen!

We hear strange theremin-type music. Mollug points.

                    MOLLUG (CONT'D)
          There it is...a fairy! Right between that beer can and
          that pumpkin.

ANGLE ON: Real beer can and real pumpkin.

ANGLE ON: Death Raider. He holds the magnifying glass up to his eye and
peers through it.

ANGLE ON: Person in FAIRY COSTUME floating between giant inflatable beer
can and inflatable pumpkin-shaped jumping house.

                    FAIRY
          Is it the ring you seek?

                    DEATH RAIDER
          Yes, yes!

ANGLE ON: R2-D2 trash-can guy, blooping and beeping.

                    FAIRY
          The ring is inside you. You must accept the almighty as
          your savior first to obtain its powers. Do you?

                    MOLLUG
          I want to. I'm tired of living in a swamp full of deceit
          and lies.

                    DEATH RAIDER
        I do too. I want to go to heaven when I die, and sing
        and pray all day.

                    FAIRY
        Good. If you do that, then you can become anything you
        want to be, as you walk in the footsteps of the Lord
        most high.

MUSIC: Cheesy organ

All of the characters laugh warmly, Artie-Bleep-Bloop "bleep-bloops."

A logo comes up reading: "Anointed Films Incorporated."

EXT. STREET

The assembled on-lookers are all disgusted.

                    DISGRUNTLED CUSTOMER
        See? It's not even teenagers doing a shitty dress-up
        version of blockbusters, it's a cheesy Christian
        version.

The Korean Street Vendor fesses up.

                    KOREAN STREET VENDOR
                (losing his accent)
        I know, I know. Guys, geez. Come on. Cut me some slack.
        Do you know how hard it is to trick people into seeing
        Christian movies? I'm dying out here.

Bob and David feel bad for him, but . . .

                    DAVID
        Sorry, not biting today, I'm a Science-ologist!

                    KOREAN STREET VENDOR
        Oh, I have *Battlefield Earth*—the original!

                    DAVID
        No, no, a Science-ologist, it's very different than
        Scientology. We believe all that Xenu stuff happened

seventy trillion years ago, that's a five-trillion year difference...they're just being absurd.

> BOB
> Come on, let's get those physicals!

INT. DOCTOR'S OFFICE, WAITING AREA

Various SAD CASES wait for a doctor. One BEVERLY HILLS LADY is at the desk talking to the nurse.

> BEVERLY HILLS LADY
> Yes, I would like to get more work done on my face.

> NURSE
> Can you be more specific?

> BEVERLY HILLS LADY
> Yes. I'd like to look like...Kathy Griffin.

The nurse nods and pulls up a chart for the Lady.

> NURSE
> Here, take this chart, it shows the eleven stages of Kathy Griffin...just circle one.

Camera follows the Beverly Hills Lady to the waiting area where we land on Bob and David waiting. David is reading a magazine. Bob is annoyed.

> BOB
> David, we just need physicals, we only have 'til five o'clock. Why do we have to wait for some special doctor?

> DAVID
> Bob, it's totally worth it. These guys are the best Doctors in Hollywood.

David points and we see an Oscar-like statue reading: "D, B, and T, Best Hollywood Doctors."

> BOB
> No David...it says "Best Hollywood Doctors."

>   DAVID
> Uh...yeah, *in Hollywood*.

>   RECEPTIONIST
> Ginny Burkins?

GINNY, a nervous young woman, crosses into doctor's office.

                                              CUT TO:

INT. DOCTOR'S OFFICE

GINNY enters the Doctor's office, its walls lined with certificates, awards, and actors' headshots. The DOCTOR is on the phone, distractedly listening, not writing it down...

>   DOCTOR
>   (on the phone)
> Yeah...brain tumor, cysts, sure, fever...it's done,
> I got it all, I wrote it down...it's fine, don't worry
> about it, I got it covered. No, I wrote it all down.
> Well those guys are assholes. Bye.

He hangs up and turns to Ginny, speaking quickly, cutting her off at every turn—

                      DOCTOR (CONT'D)
What is it? What do you want?

                      GINNY
I heard you were the best Doctor in Hollywood.

                      DOCTOR
Yeah, yeah, yeah, what do you got for me?

                      GINNY
Well, last summer I was diagnosed with—

                      DOCTOR
Uh-huh, uh-huh.

                      GINNY
—stomach cancer and I went for further tests—

                      DOCTOR
Uh-huh, uh-huh.

                      GINNY
And there's still—

                      DOCTOR
Done!

She stops talking.

                      DOCTOR (CONT'D)
Done, taken care of. It's gone. Don't worry about it.

                      GINNY
What . . . ?

                      DOCTOR
I'll make a call. Forget that . . .
       (shouting out his open door)
Sharon, get the O.R. on the phone, taking the stomach out. Now!

                    GINNY
          Wait...no, I mean...I don't want surgery.

                    DOCTOR
          You want a water.

                    GINNY
          No. I don't have stomach cancer. The tests came out
          negative.

                    DOCTOR
          Yeah, yeah, yeah, fine, I can work with that, no
          problem. Keep your stomach. Let me get Doctor Wilson in
          here, pitch it to him, okay?
                    (shouting out the door)
          Sharon! Get Drs. Wilson and Melchowitz in here, pronto!
                    (to Ginny)
          You don't want a water, Kombucha? Nothing. Fine.

TWO DOCTORS, WILSON and MELCHOWITZ, enter and immediately start kissing ass.

                    DOCTOR (CONT'D)
Doctors, this is Ginny Rosemont. She's going to get her
stomach taken care of here.

                    WILSON
Great.

                    MELCHOWITZ
It's exciting.

                    GINNY
Well, it's not my stomach.

                    DOCTOR
Okay, we can work with that, right guys?

                    WILSON
Yup.

                    GINNY
The pain persisted, though, and it traveled into my
intestine...

                    DOCTOR
Fine. Stop. I get it. I get where you're going and I love
it. Am I alone?

                    WILSON
I think it's great, yeah.

                    MELCHOWITZ
I see it.

                    DOCTOR
          (shouting out the door again)
Sharon, prep O.R., all three of us! We're going in now!
This is our number one priority for the rest of the day,
this is what we're working on!

                    GINNY
But I—

Doctor's phone rings. He picks it up.

                  DOCTOR

What? Uh-huh. Sick? Fuck that disease. You don't need that. I don't see you with that disease. That's not a good fit. That disease is an asshole. Head straight for the O.R. Shh, shh...It's my only priority, bye.

He turns back to Ginny and the other two Doctors.

                DOCTOR (CONT'D)

Okay, what are we doing here? Are we good here? Are we done? Ginny will validate your parking.

                GINNY

I'm Ginny.

                DOCTOR

Yup, got it. What? What?

                WILSON

Done.

                MELCHOWITZ

I love it.

The Doctors hurriedly leave. Ginny, completely overwhelmed and disarmed, watches them go...

Camera pulls out to ext. of building.

MUSIC: Heartrending, we sit on Ginny, alone...

EXT. DOCTOR'S OFFICE, HOLLYWOOD BLVD

Bob and David enter frame, and walk along, looking at their physical forms.

                BOB

I'm in tip-top shape for moviemaking.

                DAVID

Me, too, clean bill of health, and according to this I haven't done drugs for six months.

                    BOB
          I think you have mine.

They exchange forms. Bob's cell phone rings, he checks it.

                    BOB (CONT'D)
          Oh, it's my wife.

He answers the phone, and becomes wildly argumentative.

                    BOB (CONT'D)
          Yes?! What?! I don't know! No! Of course! Fine! Love you!

Bob hangs up.

                    DAVID
               (warily)
          How's that going?

                    BOB
               (ferociously)
          Great! Get off my back!!

                    DAVID
          Hey, hey, all right.

                    BOB
               (suddenly calm)
          You really should get married. It changes your life.

                    DAVID
               (upset)
          I've tried, Bob. Remember.

Bob nods, off his thoughtful look we—

                                              DISSOLVE TO:

INT. NICE RESTAURANT

BOB and his wife, NAOMI, sit at a table in this very nice restaurant.

                    BOB
          David should be here any minute.

                    NAOMI
        What's this girl's name again?

                    BOB
        I don't know, it's Lilly or Lana or something. He met
        her like, two weeks ago, and now they're getting married
        already. It seems pretty crazy.

                    NAOMI
        Let's just be happy for him.

                    BOB
        I am, I mean, I heard she's hot, so...
            (Bob's eyes widen)
        Holy shit...is that her?

David, in suit and tie and sporting a full head of hair, enters with his
fiancée LETHA BOMBZ, a stripper wearing stripper clothes, looking very
hot.

                    DAVID
        Hey, guys, I want you to meet my fiancée, Letha. Letha,
        this is Bob and Naomi. Guys, Letha Bombz.

                    BOB
        Wow! Nice to meet you.

                    DAVID
        Yeah, we're so happy, we're just bursting.

                    LETHA
        I'm happy, too. He's my favorite.

                    NAOMI
        Oh. So, "Letha Bombz," that's an interesting name.
        What nationality are you?

                    LETHA
        Oh, yeah, I'm studying to be a veterinarian or a lawyer.
        I'm so into David, though, he says he's going to put me
        through veterinarian college or lawyer school.

                    NAOMI
        Great. So, where did you guys meet?

              LETHA
At the club.

              DAVID
Yeah, The Salty Unicorn, it was really magical. We met
and danced for like, three...hundred dollars. It was
really very special.

              BOB AND NAOMI
Yeah/Sounds special.

              WAITER
           (to David and Letha)
Madame, Monsieur, can I get you a cocktail?

Letha checks out the wine list.

              LETHA
Yeah, do you have a room where I can get champagne?

              WAITER
I can bring you champagne in this room.

              LETHA
I'd like a glass of champagne, then. Oh, and can it cost
thirty dollars, please?

The confused Waiter nods.

              LETHA (CONT'D)
Oh, I've gotta go. You stay right here. I'll be right
back in a minute.

She kisses David on the cheek.

              NAOMI
Are you going to the bathroom?

              LETHA
           (confusedly)
No.

Letha leaves.

                    DAVID
      Oh my God, you guys, she's awesome! Isn't she awesome?

Bob and Naomi swallow their doubts.

                    NAOMI
      She's great.

                    BOB
      Hey, buddy...uh, you have no problem with her being a
      stripper?

                    DAVID
        (laughs)
      She's not a stripper, Bob, she's a dancer. Big
      difference. Huge. It's a new millennium, get with it. I
      just want you guys to be happy for me.

                BOB AND NAOMI
      We are...yeah...

Letha returns to the table, sweaty, sipping a water, like she just got
offstage from dancing.

                    LETHA
        (surprised to see David)
      Oh, you're still here! What's going on?

David stands up and puts an arm around her, she gently removes it, but he
doesn't seem to care.

                    DAVID
      We were just talking...about us.

David and Letha turn to go.

                    BOB
      So, aren't you guys having dinner?

                    DAVID
      Oh, I can't, Bob, I'm so in love I'm not hungry. All I
      can eat are chocolate Santas.

                          BOB
          Well, I guess you're really in love.

                          DAVID
          Yup. It's great.

Bob and Naomi watch them go.

                                        DISSOLVE TO:

EXT. SMALL-TOWN MAIN STREET

MUSIC: Scored throughout, like a '70s cheap horror film, *The Stepford Wives*

Dolly down Main street of a perfect Disney/David Lynch small town. Couples pass camera, *none with kids*. All the women are super-hot stripper types, all the men are pasty, slovenly, nerdy guys.

                          DAVID (V.O.)
          So, we got married and moved into a quaint little
          town that Letha knew about. There were lots of other
          couples there, and they had free peanuts at the street
          corners, speakers in the trees, and a free brunch
          every day.

ANGLE ON: Speaker in tree. Hot, pumping stripper-rock playing.

End on small town sign: "Welcome to Cheetah's III, pop. 346" beside a liquor license.

                          DAVID (V.O.)
          It was great. The years went by, and Letha really did
          make me feel special . . .

MUSIC: The stripper rock song playing on the town speakers becomes louder, more present as it underscores—

A MONTAGE

INT. SUBURBAN HOUSE

NOTE—The following montage is staged in a camera lock-off position. A picture window shows seasonal changes outside.

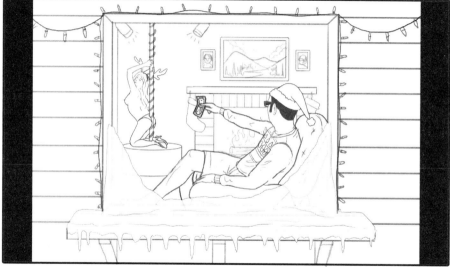

David sits in a recliner, watching as Letha dances, peeling off panties and bras, and tossing them to David, who smells them and sets them aside in an ever-growing pile. David's hair thins as the years go on, fall passes, decorations give way to a—christmas tree in the corner. Letha doing a table dance just for David, there's money all around her, and David throws more. This is replaced by a full-frame of a

GRAPHIC: A FIRST ANNIVERSARY CARD

...it opens as it wipes screen and we hear Letha's voice reading the inscription..

                    LETHA (V.O.)
         To a very special guy....

Then we are back in the lock-off camera outside the same house. Inside, a birthday celebration. David sits in the same chair, birthday paper hat on his head. Letha dances.

                    LETHA(V.O.)
         You're my favorite...

We DISSOLVE AGAIN to the lock-off shot outside the house—colorful leaves on the tree, panties in the corner piled high.

>   LETHA (V.O.)
>   You're so nice, and sweet, and funny, and um...God,
>   these fucking heels are killing me. My shoes hurt...

She pulls him into a jello pit in the center of their living room. A BOUNCER in referee outfit watches, after which we DISSOLVE TO:

A SEVENTH ANNIVERSARY CARD, and as we see Letha's personal inscription...we hear her voice.

>   LETHA (V.O.)
>   (her inscription)
>   Anyway, you're so sweet and...wait, you're David,
>   right?

>   DAVID (V.O.)
>   I guess I was pretty happy, but one day I had to see the
>   mayor about a discrepancy in my bill...

END MONTAGE

EXT. CITY HALL

Small-town city hall building.

EXT. THE OUTER DOOR OF THE MAYOR'S OFFICE

POV: A sign reads, "The Honorable Jimmy B., Mayor." The door opens, revealing...an office as cluttered and dark as the office in a nightclub. MAYOR JIMMY B. sits behind a desk, with piles of cash on it. A BOUNCER stands behind him. Jimmy counts cash. He looks up to see David, timidly standing before him, holding his bill—

>   MAYOR
>   What's up, kid?

>   DAVID
>   Oh, sorry to interrupt. It's about my champagne bill, I
>   don't remember ordering—

The Mayor interrupts.

> MAYOR
> Look kid, you having a good time here?

> DAVID
> Sure.

> MAYOR
> Okay good, when people come to my town I want them to
> have a good time. (to Bouncer) Cappy, give the kid a
> V.I.P. pass. (getting up) All right? We square? That'll
> get you free parking and a discount on sexy tomatoes.
> I gotta go see a man about a horse. (beat) For real. A
> real horse. I don't gotta pee.

They watch David leave, then the Mayor nods to the Bouncer. They walk
through an unmarked door behind the Mayor's desk. A beat. Then David
reenters the office.

> DAVID
> If I could just...

David notices the secret door is ajar. He watches through the opening.

David's P.O.V.

INT. STRIP CLUB LOCKER ROOM

We see the town's WIVES, standing by lockers in various stages of undress.
Jimmy B. takes control.

> MAYOR
> All right girls, gather 'round. Let's go over the
> monthlies. Devin St. Pierre, Devin St. Luscia, Letha...

ANGLE ON: Letha, dressed as "The Wife," takes off her blond wig and
dresses in a stripper outfit.

ANGLE ON: Eavesdropping David, confused...

> MAYOR (CONT'D)
> Devin St. Devin...

                    LETHA
Call us by our real names, Jimmy.

                    MAYOR
Okay, Cindy.

David is appalled.

                    MAYOR (CONT'D)
One of your husbands was just bugging me about his
champagne bill, and it wasn't even that high.

                    LETHA
Which one? Was it Henry, the bald guy with the toupee?
You should kick him out of town, I think he's running
out of money.

                    MAYOR
Nah. It's one of the other ones. The dark-haired one.

                    LETHA
The little gayish one? Kinda jewy. Smells like old cans?

                    MAYOR
Yeah.

                    LETHA
That's David. I can pump him for an extra couple of
bottles a week. I know I can, Jimmy.

                    MAYOR
Well get to it.

PUSH IN: on horrified David.

                    MAYOR (O.S.) (CONT'D)
Okay listen, we're opening up a new town, so I need you
ladies to get some new husbands. Now get out there and
shake your ass!

SMASH CUT TO:

INT. DINER

David is passionately addressing other HUSBANDS: HUTCH, DEAN, and TODD.

> DAVID
> I'm telling you! I saw it with my own eyes! Hutch, I saw
> your wife, Devin, take off her wig and...

> HUTCH
> Wig? My wife doesn't have a wig!

> DAVID
> And her name isn't Devin, it's Tina. And Dean, I heard
> your wife say that her OTHER husbands are buying more
> champagne than you!

> DEAN
> Other husbands? I'm her only husband.

> DAVID
> How can you be sure?

> DEAN
> Because she tells me! Every night she tells me I'm the best guy she's met all night!

> KEN
> My wife tells me the exact same thing!

> TODD
> My wife does...too...

They realize how strange this is...

> HUTCH
> David, whatever you're saying, it's just paranoia, man.

> DAVID
> Oh yeah? Ask yourselves, have you ever had sex with your wives? Ever?

No answer...They look at each other, at the ground...

> DAVID (CONT'D)
> Have you? Have you...

                                                      CUT TO:

EXT. STEPS OF CITY HALL

CLOSE ON: David, loudly ranting—

> DAVID (O.C.)
> (shouting)
> Have any of you ever had sex with your wives? Huh?

DOLLY BACK to reveal David on city hall steps speaking to a small mob of HUSBANDS.

> DAVID (CONT'D)
> Because it's a lie, gentlemen! You're not special! You're not different from all the other guys in town! You're being played for suckers!

                    VOICE IN THE CROWD
Not me!

                    DAVID
Oh, yeah, answer my question: Have you ever had sex with
your wife?!

A couple Husbands raise their hands.

                    DAVID (CONT'D)
And lap dances don't count!

All hands go down, except for TODD.

                    TODD
Um, what if you come in your pants?

                    DAVID
No!

Todd's hand goes down.

>   DAVID (CONT'D)
> Ask yourself, have you ever heard of a town with a
> cover charge?! Jim, haven't you ever noticed, you have
> the same wife as Tony. Different wig. Have you ever had
> your two wives together? No! They're stringing us along,
> guys!

Jimmy B. and two GOONS watch from across the street.

>   JIMMY B.
> What the hell is going on?

They take in David for a beat.

>   DAVID
> It's a lie, gentlemen! A lie! This whole town is a lie!

One of the Goons reaches inside his coat for a gun, but Jimmy stops him,
"be cool."

>   DAVID (CONT'D)
> Listen, we can leave here, find real wives to marry, who
> would have sex with us!

>   MONTY
> Would they be hot?

>   DAVID
> No, not like these wives, no. But they'd love you, for
> real, and they'd be pretty...on the inside!

David is losing them...

>   DAVID (CONT'D)
> And it wouldn't just be about your money! It'd be about
> who you are as a person!

>   HUTCH
> Wait a second, go back, they're not as hot?

>   DEAN
> They wouldn't wear just underwear all the time?

                   DAVID

No, of course not! They wouldn't wear underwear all the time! But they'd love you . . .

                 KEN (JIMMY KIMMEL)

Would they dance for us while we watched football?

                 DAVID
                   (really angry)

NO!! These would be real, independent women, with their own ideas, and identities, and ambitions!

A long pause, the Husbands mutter amongst themselves.

                 MONTY

I'm gonna stay here.

                 DEAN

Yeah, me too.

ANGLE ON: Jimmy B. and Goons, smiling. They nod to each other and head off.

ANGLE ON: David, dumbfounded.

                 DAVID

What?

The Husbands wander off, chattering . . .

                 HUSBANDS CHATTER

It's okay! / I kinda figured it out a while ago. / Me, too! / I'm cool with it.

David is left on the steps, alone, as the crowd disperses. CRANE SHOT rises as David falls to his knees.

                 DAVID
                   (screaming)

Noooooooo!

DISSOLVE TO:

EXT. RESTAURANT, SIDEWALK SEATING

ANGLE ON: A JAMES CAMERON GUY at a table with STUDIO GUY in a sharp suit.

               CAMERON
          (acting)
    "Nooooooo!"

              STUDIO GUY
Great, hero on his knees, all alone. Sounds like you've
got an ending. Now, let's hear about the beginning.

               CAMERON
Okay, that's all I've got on that one...an ending.

              STUDIO GUY
Mm. All right, well, you're the master. Everyone at the
studio is so happy with your work. I mean, your last

movie was truly a titanic success, we just think you're the king of the world, and we want whatever you got next.

> CAMERON
> I got nothin'.

> STUDIO GUY
> Fine, we're in.

A beat. Their food arrives.

> STUDIO GUY (CONT'D)
> Seriously, though, maybe we can brainstorm, you know, while we eat.

Cameron nods.

ANGLE ON: Bob and David being seated behind James Cameron as they are handed menus.

> BOB
> Wow, this place is nice.

> DAVID
> Oh, Bob, this is *the* hot place to eat-and-be-seen-eating in La-La-Land.

> BOB
> Wow, look at all these stupid showbiz assholes.

A glimpse of various Hollywood shmoozer couples. Don Simpson/Jennifer Garner pair. Courtney Love/Gay hairdresser, etc.

> DAVID
> Yeah, it's pretty cool, huh?

> BOB
> Yeah.

Bob takes out a pen to write on a napkin.

> BOB (CONT'D)
> Okay, so...what's our concept?

                DAVID
Huh?

                BOB
For our movie. The lady said we had to get a concept for
the film, remember?

                DAVID
        (distractedly reading menu)
A twenty-dollar hot dog?

ANGLE ON: David's menu, one item: "Le Hot Dog . . . 20 dollars"

ANGLE ON: Bob, mulling David's statement.

                BOB
Hm. A movie about a twenty-dollar hot dog? Okay, okay,
that'd be like "In a world turned upside down, where hot
dogs are twenty dollars . . ."

ANGLE ON: James Cameron Guy slurping soup, a thoughtful look on his face.

                CAMERON
I think I've got something. For the new movie. Just came
to me.

                STUDIO GUY
I'm listening.

                CAMERON
Upside-down world. If the world turned upside down.

                STUDIO GUY
The whole world? That would be inside-out, then, right?

                CAMERON
        (dismayed)
Oh. Yeah. Never mind.

ANGLE ON: Bob and David.

                BOB
". . . one man fights for the last hot dog!"

David looks up from his menu.

> DAVID
>
> What?

> BOB
>
> I was riffing on your hot dog idea.

> DAVID
>
> No, no, they have a hot dog, on the menu, for twenty dollars. A New York–style hot dog.

> BOB
>
> Oh. New York–style? Cool.

ANGLE ON: James Cameron Guy and Studio Guy.

> CAMERON
>
> Okay...okay...got a cool idea. What if it's just New York? *Upside-down New York!*

> STUDIO GUY
>
> Huh?

> CAMERON
>
> Yeah, yeah...some kind of gravitational flux causes the city to flip, and people are fighting for...CEILING SPACE!

> STUDIO GUY
>
> It's great. That's a great title.

The Studio Guy excitedly takes notes.

> CAMERON
>
> Better one: *New York, York New!*

> STUDIO GUY
>
> Now we got two!

ANGLE ON: Bob and David, ordering from the waiter...

> BOB
>
> ...and I'll take the ten-dollar oatmeal bucket.

Waiter takes their menus.

> DAVID
>
> Dude, let's totally do an underground movie, with real street cred, 'cause all these big bombs just make me mad, man.

ANGLE ON: James Cameron Guy and Studio Guy.

> CAMERON
>
> Okay...how about this, a madman is dropping bombs, big bombs, on the streets, and people have to go underground to save themselves...?

> STUDIO GUY
>
> Yeah, yeah...

ANGLE ON: Bob and David eating massive hot dogs. Bob talks through a mouthful of food.

> BOB
>
> ...so, you know, I told you about my favorite shirt, right?

> DAVID
>
> That ancient blue thing?

> BOB
>
> Yeah. I lost a button on it, and I'm like so pissed. If I don't find that button it's over, the end of the world, for that shirt.

> DAVID
>
> Damn.

ANGLE ON: James Cameron Guy and Studio Guy.

> CAMERON
>
> Yeah...yeah, so they have to find this ancient button, and press it, to reverse gravity, or it's the end of the world.

> STUDIO GUY
>
> Great! This is great stuff!

ANGLE ON: David and Bob finishing their hot dogs.

> DAVID
> Yeah . . . so last night the Angels game was on, also the
> Devils were playing, so it was like the ultimate battle
> with my roommate for the remote control.

> BOB
> That dick? He acts like he's the last guy on earth.

ANGLE ON: James Cameron Guy and Studio Guy.

> CAMERON
> . . . and so then, our hero, "Dick" . . . the last man on
> earth, has to battle Angels . . . *and Devils* in a remote—

ANGLE ON: Bob and David.

> BOB
> Too bad you can't change the setting on your remote to
> "stun."

David laughs at this lame joke.

ANGLE ON: James Cameron Guy and Studio Guy.

> CAMERON
> . . . a *remote* . . . set-ting.

ANGLE ON: Bob and David have finished their hot dogs/oatmeal buckets.

> DAVID
> Great oatmeal. How much is this gonna cost?

ANGLE ON: Studio Guy.

> STUDIO GUY
> Wait a second, what's the price tag on this thing?

ANGLE ON: Bob, slurping the last bit of oatmeal.

> BOB
> Let's see that bill.

Bob looks at it...

> BOB (CONT'D)
> Ninety-one dollars?

ANGLE ON: James Cameron Guy.

> CAMERON
> I don't know, upside-down New York...91 million?

> STUDIO GUY
> (taken aback)
> Ahhh...I don't know. It's a bit pricey.

ANGLE ON: Bob Guy feels bad about the bill.

> BOB
> I don't know...

> DAVID
> No, man, you're holding it upside down.

Bob flips it over and is pleasantly surprised.

> BOB
> Got it—

ANGLE ON: James Cameron Guy.

> CAMERON
> I got it! Turn the camera *upside down*. Shoot it in New
> York.

> STUDIO GUY
> That we can do!

ANGLE ON: Bob, looking at the bill right side up now.

> BOB
> That's much better.

> DAVID
> Cool. You pay, I gotta go take a dump.

                    BOB
That's great to hear. I'll spread the word!

ANGLE ON: Studio Guy to Cameron, excitedly—

                    STUDIO GUY
Great. I can't wait to tell the world about your next
piece of shit...oops!

                                                    CUT TO:

EXT. HOLLYWOOD BLVD.

Bob and David walking down the street.

                    BOB
Well, we still need a concept for our movie.

                    DAVID
Yeah.

                    BOB
Okay, so, like what are your favorite films? Name a few.

                    DAVID
It's hard to say...I've still never seen a movie.

                    BOB
Well, there's our problem right there. We should see a
movie.

A WOMAN approaches with a clipboard that reads "Free movie tickets."

                    WOMAN
Free movie tickets! Would you like to see a screening of
a new movie?

                    DAVID
Check it out. Our prayers are answered.

INT. MOVIE THEATRE - CONTINUOUS

Bob and David enter the screening and find seats in the back. An energetic, overly cheerful TESTER gets everyone's attention at the front of the theatre.

>   TESTER
>   Okay, everybody in? Come down to the front.

Bob and David remain in the back.

>   TESTER (CONT'D)
>   We're going to show you some scenes from a new film,
>   a work in progress. Then we'll have a free-form
>   discussion. And afterwards, there is free pizza, as
>   promised. Just to make sure, you're all boys between the
>   ages of thirteen and eighteen, right?

They are all teenage boys, wearing rock T-shirts, looking like slobs and a little awkward.

>   TESTER (CONT'D)
>   Great, we really think you'll enjoy this, because it's a
>   movie about stock car racing.

ANGLE ON: The boys are excited, a few high fives.

>   TESTER (CONT'D)
>   Its working title is *Raging Racers*.

Theatre goes dark as we see on the screen:

Title: "Clips from 'Raging Racers'" (NOTE: THIS FILM IS A PARODY/HOMAGE TO BAZ LUHRMANN, LIKE *MOULIN ROUGE*, SO PICTURE IT THAT WAY, SATURATED COLORS, OVERBLOWN EVERYTHING.)

EXT. TRAILER PARK

Wide shot of nastiest, rusted-out trailer home. A beater car is parked in front, we can faintly see a phantom of a number on the hood of the beater, like it's been raced in a demolition derby. A scraggly dog bellows sadly.

SFX: In a circle in the corner of the screen, a greasy looking PIT CREW CHIEF addresses us.

>   PIT CREW CHIEF
>   This here's the story of Danni Maqueef, the greatest car
>   racer the South has ever seen.

Intense POST-EFFECT push-in through trailer-home window...

INT. TRAILER HOME

A cluttered, threadbare home. DANNI, a six-year old girl with pigtails,
each tied with ribbons, one blue, one pink, kneels on the gross shag
carpeting playing with Matchbox cars.

SFX: Real racetrack sounds.

>   PIT CREW CHIEF
>   There's Danni, right now she's just a kid. That's right,
>   *she*. It's Danni with an "I." Uh-oh, here comes her
>   father, the widower "Stumpy" Haskins.

SWISH PAN to the door violently swinging open. Quick push in on "STUMPY."
He is drunk, has stump legs (*Dorf on Golf*), with garish *Moulin Rouge*-style
makeup, and waves a bottle of Mad Dog.

>   STUMPY
>   (yelling) Danni! Where the hell's the who what for?

The DOG on the bottle of wine comes to life and barks.

>   MAD DOG
>   Arf! Arf! Arf! Arf!

Stumpy barks back at it, scaring it.

>   STUMPY
>   Graarrff!!
>   (sees Danni playing with cars)
>   Goddammit. Put those cars away! You're a girl! You
>   should be doing girl things!

Danni breaks into tears.

>   DANNI
>   If girls can't race, then I don't wanna be a girl!

Animated question marks appear over Stumpy's head accompanied by bubbly
sounds.

> STUMPY
> What are you saying?

> DANNI
> I'm gonna cut my hair!

She runs down the hall. HANDHELD CAMERA runs backward with her, into the
bathroom, and the door slams shut before Stumpy can get a foot in it.

INT. BATHROOM

Danni looks in the mirror where a racing card of Giles "Studs" Manly Sr.
comes to life and tells her...

> STUDS MANLEY
> Follow your dreams!

She picks up a pair of scissors and cuts off her pigtails. Stumpy bangs on
the door.

> STUMPY (O.C.)
> Don't you cut your pigtails, young lady!

His head bursts through and the camera swirls up and into his sputtering
mouth.

> STUMPY (CONT'D) (O.C.)
> You'll never be a racing person or fall in loooooooove!

She tosses her pigtails into the toilet and flushes. The toilet flush
handle ignites the sound of...

SFX: A Drag Racer Engine...

As the colorful pigtails swirl around in the water, they transform
into...

EXT. RACETRACK, OVERHEAD SHOT

A bright BLUE RACE CAR and a BRIGHT YELLOW CAR zipping around the track.

Graphic: "TWENTY YEARS LATER"

Camera ZOOMS down (post-effect) into frontage of dusty racetrack...
according to the weatherbeaten sign (with colorful balloon-letters) it's
the "Camptown Racetrack (5 Miles Long)"

As the camera dollies past happy workers in colorful jumpsuits, a song
begins...

All colors are oversaturated. Shooting is filled with Dutch angles, quick
cuts, maniacal laughter, and other *Moulin Rouge* b.s.

                    PIT CREW DANCERS
                (herky jerky melody)
            Camptown racers sing this song,
            Doo Dah, Doo Dah.
            Camptown racetrack five miles long
            Oh the doo dah day.
                (melody suddenly sweet)
            Gwine to love all night,
            Gwine to love all day!

The singers are interrupted by Dancer #3.

                    DANCER
          Hey it's Doo Dah!

Two guys, covered in grease, dressed in muscle-T's and sharing one pair
of pants tromp over to the gang. One guy's shirt reads, "DOO," and the
other's reads, "DAH." They do a gay dance.

                    DOO
          Look out, gang, here comes Studs Manly!

                    DAH
          The greatest race car driver in the south!

                    DOO
          In my mouth?!

ANGLE ON: TEENAGE VIEWER in theatre, confused and uncomfortable.

ON-SCREEN: An older "Stumpy" bursts out of the "office."

>   STUMPY
>   Shut up you two...or one...or...oh whatever! Danni!

INT. RACETRACK, OFFICE

Danni enters the colorful pigsty office of the track, wiping grease from her hands. She looks pretty butch.

>   DANNI
>   What is it, Pops?

>   STUMPY
>   It's your lucky day. I swore I'd never do this, but,
>   well...Studs Manly is on his way over and he needs
>   someone to race against. Dilly Chestholder is getting
>   his stomach pumped, and Bugs Vapor got his foot stuck in
>   a man, so you're all I've got.

>   DANNI
>   But I thought I couldn't 'cause I was a girl!

Stumpy shushes her and hands her a big, bushy moustache.

>   STUMPY
>   Shhh, wear this and no one will know.

CLOSE ON: Danni looking at the moustache.

A Racing Flag wipes the screen and we—

>   CUT TO:

INT. DANNI'S CAR

MUSIC throughout—

Danni with a fake moustache looks very much like a guy, though she still has lipstick on. She guns her engine and checks out STUDS in the next car. We push in to STUDS, who looks her up and down lasciviously and sneers. The closer we pull in to him the more we see that he, too, has a bit of lipstick and maybe some eyeliner on. They both talk/sing the following...

> STUDS
> Get your motor runnin'.

> DANNI
> Head out on the highway?

DOO DAH walks up between the two cars and starts the race. The race is filmed on a set with the background just a blur behind the cars.

> STUDS
> I'll be coming around the racetrack when I come.

> DANNI
> I'll be coming around the racetrack when I come.

Now they start to get more romantic, and suddenly Studs seems to have heavier makeup on, and lip gloss.

> STUDS AND DANNI TOGETHER
> We'll be comin around the racetrack, we'll be comin around the racetrack.

They leave their cars, join hands, and are whisked away up to the heavens, leaving a trail of stars behind them. They waltz around the evening sky amongst hundreds of stars.

> STUDS AND DANNI TOGETHER (CONT'D)
> We'll be coming around the racetrack when weeeeee coooome.

They gaze into each other's eyes and are about to kiss, but turn away dramatically. Studs jumps onto the smiling moon and sings—

> STUDS
> One hundred twinkling stars in the sky, one hundred twinkling stars. I take one down, (he plucks one and takes a bite of it) pass it around. (He gently places the star on Danni's chest.)

> STUDS AND DANNI TOGETHER
> Ninety-nine twinkling stars in the sky.

They gaze into each other's eyes again, are about to kiss, then both turn away dramatically. Studs breaks into an insane jig.

>   STUDS
>   Love, love the magical fruit. The more you eat it, the
>   more you toot.

Studs lightly farts and cartoon hearts float up, Danni is charmed. They lean in to kiss.

And the movie stops with a short graphic: END OF CLIP.

INT. THEATRE

LIGHTS UP as the TESTER takes the stage, clapping, alone.

>   TESTER
>   Okay, so there we go. Again, you are our target
>   audience, and so, just cut loose—what did you think
>   of it?

The teenage boys are stunned.

> TESTER (CONT'D)
> Okay...okay...let me put it this way. First of all how many of you would say you loved it? Show of hands.

No hands go up.

> TESTER (CONT'D)
> Okay, zero, that's fine. How many would say you liked it, it was "okay"?

Again, nothing.

> TESTER (CONT'D)
> None of you, fine. Now how many would say it was horrible? You just hated it.

Every hand goes up.

> TESTER (CONT'D)
> One, two, three...uhh...pretty much everyone. That's fine, by the way. Now, let's get some specifics, can anyone tell me what they didn't like about it?

The weirded-out kids grunt and scoff, shaking their heads.

> TESTER (CONT'D)
> Somebody, come on...How 'bout we start with you?

> KID #1
> It was bad.

> TESTER
> Mm-hm, anybody else?

> KID #2
> It wasn't good.

> TESTER
> Okay, little more specific, anybody?

> KID #3
> There's something wrong with it, man...

>   TESTER
>   Okaaayy, well—

KID #4 is dressed in a black T-shirt, ripped army jacket, total KISS ARMY kid.

>   KID #4
>   Guys, come on, just say it! I mean, that movie was
>   totally g—

He is interrupted by a high-pitched squeal from offscreen...

>   SCREECHING VOICE
>   I'm here!!!

In bursts JAZ LIPMANN, the film's effeminate, eccentric director.

>   TESTER
>   (to Kid #4—)
>   Hold that thought—

Jaz bursts into a rant.

>   JAZ
>   I'm here! I'm late, I know! Slap me and call me
>   sweetheart! Ugh, family business.

>   TESTER
>   Jaz? You're not supposed to be here.

>   JAZ
>   I'm so sorry. Have you shown it yet?

>   TESTER
>   Yes, I was just getting a reaction from this gentleman.

Jaz is a ball of energy, unstoppable.

>   JAZ
>   Great. I directed this piece. And wrote it, and it's a
>   story from my heart, and I want to get it right. So tell
>   me, what did you think?

                          KID #1
          Uhh...I, uhhh...

                          TESTER
          You were saying it was "totally g-" something?

                          JAZ
          "Totally g-" what? Totally g-reat, g-ripping, g—anything.
          I can totally take it, seriously, just cut loose.

                          KID #1
          Well...it was not...my kind of movie.

                          JAZ
          Okay, I'm sorry, I can't accept that. I mean, it's got
          everything. Racing, music, a hot girl. You do like girls?

Kid #2 speaks up.

                          KID #2
          There were no girls in that movie.

All the other kids murmur agreement.

                          JAZ
          Of course there were. What do you mean?

Kid #3 pipes up, confused.

                          KID #3
          Which one? It looked like two guys.

Murmurs of agreement.

                          JAZ
          Danni. You know, that's Danni with an "I" at the end—
          she's a girl. And "Studs" couldn't be more of a guy.
          I mean, you guys loved Studs, right? He's totally 100
          percent all-beef male.

                          KID #4
          The dude with lipstick?

                         JAZ
Well, he had a splash of makeup on, I mean, that's
moviemaking. What are you implying?

                         TESTER
Yeah, you know if we could just let this first young
man—
        (pointing out Kid #1)
—say his piece. What was it again? "Totally g—"?

                         JAZ
G-usto, full of gusto?

                         TESTER
Let him speak.

                         KID #1
No . . . uh, totally—
        (whispering)
—gay.
        (louder)
Totally gay.

Murmurs growing.

                         KID #2
Really gay.

                         KID #3
Not gay like "lame," but gay like, "gay."

The group agrees.

                         JAZ
Okay, okay, is this a prank or something? Where are the
cameras? I mean I'm watching a movie set at a racetrack,
with macho racers. You know what, can we show the clip
where Danni and Studs go to the oil rig that Danni works
at and they get in a macho tough-guy wrestling fight . . .
in the oil, and then sing—

All the kids interrupt with a chorus of boos.

> KIDS
>
> No! Please, no! Oooo!

> JAZ
>
> All right, all right . . . I'm just trying to understand, because, you know I, myself, am not gay. I have a wife—honey, are you in the back?

In the back of the theatre, Jaz's very DYKEY WIFE stands up and waves.

> JAZ (CONT'D)
>
> I have my babies . . . there they are.

Down the aisle we see THREE PEKINGESE DOGS.

> JAZ (CONT'D)
>
> Hi, babies! I mean, I don't understand this comment.

Kid #4 stands up.

> KID #4
>
> Could I say something?

> JAZ
>
> Please.

> KID #4
>   (matter-of-factly)
> I'm gay. Everybody knows I'm gay. Right?

> KID #3
>
> Yeah, Brad's gay. Whatever.

> KID #4
>
> Anyway, this movie is very gay, but more importantly, you are gay.

> JAZ
>
> Okay, but let's talk about the movie. You say you're gay, and you say the movie's gay, but you claim you don't like the movie. I'm as confused as a pumpkin on Christmas Day.

> KID #4
>
> Forget about the movie for a second. Do you like men?

                         JAZ
I have sex with men.

                         KID #4
Do you like it?

                         JAZ
Like it? I love it.

                         KID #4
Well, that's what being gay is. It's more than that, but
that's sort of at the core of it.

                         JAZ
          (stunned, getting emotional)
Oh. Okay. Wow. This explains so much. Well, this is
great, I've learned a lot from you fellows.

He wipes a tear.

                    JAZ (CONT'D)
          (singing)
When a boy teaches a man,
And pizza is part of the plan.
Then everybody can stand,
to lend a hand...

ANGLE ON: Bob and David in the back of the theatre.

                         DAVID
Man, I did not think that this could get any gayer.

Bob looks at David. Bob suddenly has slight lipstick and eyeliner.

                         BOB
          (talk-singing)
Think again, David!
          (singing)
There's a world beside you...inside you...

David turns away...

DAVID
I'm outta here.

ANGLE ON: Bob, his makeup is suddenly gone.

> BOB
> (not singing)
> Buddy, I was just kidding!

EXT. THEATRE

David and Bob exit, back onto Hollywood Blvd.

> BOB
> David, slow down.

> DAVID
> Bob, we've got 'til five o'clock, we can't dick around.

> BOB
> Right, so what do we need next?

> DAVID
> Movie star.

> BOB
> Shit. We can't afford a movie star. How about a future
> star?

> DAVID
> Someone who isn't born yet?

> BOB
> No, not that much in the future. Just a few years. I
> mean, we're in Hollywood. They must be everywhere. Throw
> a rock and you'll hit one.

David tosses a rock in the air and it pings off something behind them. We
hear . . .

> PERFORMER (OFFSCREEN)
> Ow! Who threw that?

Bob and David turn and look pleased—

                    BOB
            What did I tell ya?!

They see a STREET PERFORMER (played by BRIAN POSEHN!) in a Tin Man outfit,
painted completely silver, funnel on his head. A sign reads, "Tin Man
Robot Show." There is a silver hat on the ground in front of him. He moves
in a jerky motion, bending forward.

                    DAVID
            Great, huh?

                    BOB
            Wow, he's really like a robot.

                    DAVID
            Yeah, that used to be a tin man.

                    BOB
            He seems really serious.

                    DAVID
            Hey, let's give him some bucks.

Bob and David drop dollars in his hat. The Performer explodes—

> PERFORMER
> What the fuck are you putting in my hat?

> DAVID
> What . . . we gave you some money.

> PERFORMER
> Just 'cause I'm sick, I don't need your charity, asshole!

> BOB
> What charity? You're a street performer!

> PERFORMER
> No, I'm not! I'm trying to pick up my goddamned hat!

> DAVID
> Well, you're moving like a robot!

> PERFORMER
> I have arthritis.

TWO TOURISTS walk by and toss in coins. The Performer mutters . . .

> PERFORMER (CONT'D)
> Thank you.

> BOB
> What the—Wait, why are you dressed like a tin man?

> PERFORMER
> It's sunblock! I could only get it in silver, they were
> out of clear!

> DAVID
> But your jacket, everything, your shoes!

> PERFORMER
> I PUT TOO MUCH ON!

> BOB
> Why are you wearing a funnel on your head?

> PERFORMER
> (pulling the funnel off)
> God damn my roommate!

ANOTHER TOURIST drops a coin in his hat.

> PERFORMER (CONT'D)
> Thank you, sir.

> BOB
> What was that?

> DAVID
> What about the sign? Robot show?

The Performer is shocked.

> PERFORMER
> I didn't even see that fuckin' thing! Help me get my
> hat!

Bob helps The Performer get his hat. Under the hat is a cup.

> BOB
> What's this cup for?

> PERFORMER
> It's my good luck money cup. My father's father gave that
> to me before he dyed...his hair.

A WOMAN strolls by, tossing a dollar in his cup.

> PERFORMER (CONT'D)
> Thank you.

> DAVID
> What the fuck?

> BOB
> What's with the fucking money?

> PERFORMER
> That was my mom. She's giving me money so I can wash my
> clothes.

                              BOB
            You're impossible!

The Performer growls at Bob. Bob growls back. The Performer walks off in
a strange, herky-jerky manner. David taps Bob on the shoulder.

                              DAVID
            Bob, check it out.

David points to a limo pulling up to the curb.

ANGLE ON: Bob and David, the limo, and its passengers are offscreen for
the following...

                              BOB
            You think it's a movie star?

                              DAVID
            No...I recognize that guy...he's a famous film
            producer.

                              BOB
            Really? How can you tell?

                              DAVID
            Check out the Italian shoes, the hottie on his arm, and
            the ponytail. That's the giveaway.

                              BOB
            Wow! I had no idea you knew so much about filmmaking.

                              DAVID
            I read a lot of magazines.

                              BOB
            Hey, remember we need a lock of hair from a producer?

David pulls out a pair of scissors.

                              DAVID
            I'm on the case.

ANGLE ON: OREN BURG, a film producer, a HOTTIE girlfriend, and FRANK, his
accountant, all seen from behind. They approach a movie poster mounted on
a theatre wall under a banner reading: PREMIERING TONITE!

> OREN BURG
>
> This is gonna be great. The culmination of one man's brilliant vision.

> FRANK
>
> One man?

Oren ignores this. The three stare at the poster. From behind, Bob and David sneak up. Bob picks up Oren's ponytail, David snips it off, and they run. Camera doesn't move, as Oren snaps his head around.

> OREN BURG
>
> What the hell—?

FREEZE FRAME on his shocked expression.

GRAPHIC: "Film Producer, Oren Burg"

(Oren is played by David.)

MUSIC: Noodling melody, "Sugar in the Haystack," like the Grateful Dead dicking around. Studio version.

In POST, we pull in past Oren's face to the poster, and the poster is for a Woodstock type of movie called, *NOODLESTOCK!* . . . silhouettes of hippy musicians done in Day-Glo colors, crowd of hippies celebrating.

NOODLESTOCK! - DOCUMENTARY SHOT ON HI-DEF VIDEO, HANDHELD

EXT. FIELD

Overhead HELICOPTER SHOT of people arriving for music festival from all directions. A stage is set up.

> OREN BURG (V.O.)
>
> . . . it's gonna be huge. Big. Bigger than Woodstock. It's gonna make Woodstock look like a backyard barbecue for midgets.

EXT. FIELD

VARIOUS MODERN HIPPY-FOLK arriving with their sleeping bags, coolers, hippy-sticks, and smiles.

                        SINGERS (O.S.)
Sugar in the haystack
feelin' so fine
Got a bag full of feelin's
and some cockleberry wine
Take a bowl of whiskey down to the
water. Put your honey in an ol' sally
swing. Drop a bag of lemons in a
cornball pea patch.
Tell Old Man Hutch go and love
everything...

INT. PROMOTER'S OFFICE

GRAPHIC, lower third: "Three Months Earlier"

OREN BURG'S office, cluttered, rock posters cover the walls. Oren is a
super-hyperactive Bill Graham-type promoter who alternates between smoking
a cigarette, a cigar, a pipe, chews tobacco, takes bites of "cigarette pie,"
and applies nicotine patches at random throughout his monologue.

                        OREN BURG
This is gonna be great, this is gonna be big, it's gonna
make Woodstock look like the US Festival. So big that
no stadium can hold it. Maybe that's an idea—get every
stadium, join them together, make one big stadium.

FRANK, Oren's buttoned-down accountant...

                        FRANK
Oren...that's going to be usurious, flying stadiums out
to...

                        OREN BURG
Yeah, you're right. I'm just blue-skyin'. How much would
Canada cost us?

                        FRANK
Uhhh...I don't have the numbers.

                        OREN BURG
Yeah, yeah...okay, yeah...how 'bout the Grand Canyon?
Get me the Grand Canyon!
        (picks up phone)
Grand Canyon?

                    (improvises)
Frank rolls his eyes...

INT. OFFICE

Frank holds up a rough poster, filled with band names, etc.

                         OREN BURG
               What's this? What the hell is this?

                         FRANK
               Well, Oren, I got the crew to pull an all-nighter, and we
               came up with a, well, just look at it...

The poster is written in Peter Max–style lettering. Oren reads it...

                         OREN
               "Noodlestock"...One Farmer's Field—three days of
               song...Thirty bands..."Reunited Phish," "String
               Cheese Incident," "Deep Banana Blackout," "Flibberty
               Jibbets and Wood," and headliners..."The Spaghetti Fish
               Accident" headlining...

Oren grins...

                         OREN BURG
               I like it...it's big...it's me...Let's go find a field.

EXT. RUNDOWN CRAFTSMAN HOUSE

CLOSE ON SIGNS: "Bless This Mess" and "Trespassing Encouraged"

INT. BAND HOUSE

Living room filled with ratty couches, beat-up Victorian furniture,
swatches of velvet hanging from walls, Persian rugs. Instruments—bongos,
guitars, sitars—and five band members (though you can only see one of
them; the others blend in to the couches, etc.—like the girl in *Snatch*);
FLOOD, GYPSY, WHEAT, BARTHOLOMEW, and AMBER. FLOOD holds out the rough
poster Oren was looking at in the last scene—

GRAPHIC: Band member names appear as they speak.

NOODLESTOCK

3 DAYS OF

CORPORATE SPONSORSHIP
ENERGY BARS & MUSIC

THE SPAGHETTI FISH ACCIDENT
STRING CHEESE INCIDENT · DEEP BANANA BLACKOUT
FLIBBERTY JIBBETS AND WOOD · RE-UNITED PHISH · SMILES FOR MYLES
SUNSHINE OVERDRIVE · THE FELT ANTLER EXPERIENCE · GUNDERSON'S FISH FLAKES
GRAMPA'S SWEATER · NOVEMBER: THE BAND · MACRAME LIGHTNING · ICE CREAM SATURDAY
GRAMPA'S CHAIR · SANDMAN'S LAMENT SLEEP TRAIN · MONKEY'S COUSIN · GRAMMA'S CHAIR · AUNTIE'S CHAIR

*LOCALLY SOURCED, FARM TO TABLE, COLD PRESSED LINSEED OIL BALLS **THE WORD MUSIC IS SUBJECTIVE AND NOT UP TO MERRIAM WEBSTER DICTIONARY STANDARDS

>   FLOOD
> I think Oren is on to something. What do you say,
> gentlemen? Everybody up for a fest?

Rising out of a couch comes...GYPSY.

>   GYPSY
> Yeah, man, I love to noodle...

From inside a sleeping bag on an indoor hammock pops WHEAT.

>   WHEAT
> Yeah...I'm there. All I need are my banana pills and my
> sleepin' hat.

From a beanbag chair BARTHOLOMEW emerges.

>   BARTHOLOMEW
> Count me in.

A bathroom door creaks open and AMBER, a super-hippy sitting on the
toilet, announces—

>   AMBER
> Hey, I made this thing into a bong.

She holds out some strange appliance rigged with duct tape.

>   WHEAT
> That already was a bong.

>   AMBER
> I guess I re-bonged it, then.

INT. THE FISH HOUSE - LATER

Everybody jams a song...improvised, maybe a drum circle!

EXT. FIELD

An Amish farmer stands by, slightly annoyed, as Oren stomps around his
farm, pointing...

                  OREN BURG
What do you want for this field? What do you want?
Batteries? Beard wax? What'll he take, Frank?

                  FRANK
Well, Mr. Odlin said his field is not for rent.

                  OREN BURG
That's bullshit! Everybody's got a price! I can't do
deals out here in the sun, it's killin' me. Gimme your
hat...

Oren grabs the farmer's hat and puts it on, then storms off. Frank shrugs
to the farmer...

INT. STRIP CLUB

Oren is hungrily watching strippers, masturbating offscreen, taking
money from Frank to put in g-strings, and talking to the Amish farmer who
doesn't watch the girls or drink.

                  OREN BURG
This is more like it. This is where deals get made. I like
you Gerd, you're Amish. You got a real Amish-ey quality to
you. And I respect your people. I was considerin' being
Amish. When I got out of college. When you're a kid, you
do crazy things. I ended up buyin' fireworks. I see you,
there but for the grace of God, y'know...

Oren looks down at the girl giving him head...

               OREN BURG (CONT'D)
Sweetheart, don't ignore the philberts.

He turns to the Amish Farmer.

               OREN BURG (CONT'D)
So, we got a deal?

EXT. FIELD

OVERHEAD SHOT - Helicopter

Trucks arriving, stage going up . . . fairly empty.

GRAPHIC: "Odlin's Field, 2 Days Til Fest"

EXT. FIELD

WORKERS loading in stages, etc. A TRAILER OFFICE.

INT. TRAILER OFFICE

Oren, Frank, 2 EMPLOYEES, working in this makeshift office.

> OREN BURG
> (loud, angry)
> Give me hard numbers here! I want hard numbers!

> FRANK
> Well, projections, including payback, out of pocket,
> merch, food/beverage . . . approximately five hundred
> grand.

No reaction from Oren.

> FRANK (CONT'D)
> Profit.

Still no reaction.

> FRANK (CONT'D)
> That's net . . . after everything. All in—

> OREN BURG
> (breaks out in big laughs)
> Hahaha . . . That's funny.

Oren stands up and begins pacing around the conference table, very
unnerving, intimidating.

> OREN BURG (CONT'D)
> See I started working to make money. I'm weird that way.
> Big money. Look, we're gonna cut costs here. My mom's
> sick, she doesn't have long, and I promised her a space
> shuttle. Now, I'm getting her that space shuttle!

>   FRANK
>   Okay . . . so . . .

>   OREN BURG
>   *Okay, so,* let's make some cuts.

EXT. FIELD

Oren and Frank walk through the backstage area, around ROADIES setting up
the stage.

>   OREN BURG
>   Two hundred porto-lets?! Two hundred?

>   FRANK
>   Well, what else? People can't just . . . poop anywhere—

>   OREN BURG
>   It's a fuckin' farm, numbnuts! You're *supposed* to shit on
>   it! That's where food comes from!

An ASSISTANT comes in with some papers for Oren.

>   OREN BURG (CONT'D)
>   Bottled water? You know how much those water companies
>   charge for packaging? No! Dig a fucking hole down to the
>   water, pump it up, get a ladle, hook it to the side of
>   the well, and charge five bucks a scoop! Next.

>   TIME CUT TO:

EXT. SAME, BACKSTAGE

>   FRANK
>   . . . the issue of power.

>   OREN BURG
>   The bands gets electricity, don't worry about the
>   audience—just give them a couple glowsticks. No!
>   Fireflies! Fly in a bunch of fireflies!

>   DISSOLVE TO:

INT. TRAILER OFFICE

Oren is checking out the finished poster. Silence as the assembled
Employees await his next screaming fit.

> OREN BURG
> Do we really need thirty bands?

No one knows how to respond to this...

> FRANK
> Oren...what? It's a festival. It's tomorrow, I mean...

> OREN BURG
> Right, right...

> FRANK
> You booked it, so...

> OREN BURG
> Yeah. Yeah, everything's cool. Everybody go home now to
> your mommies, I gotta go hold up my end of some BJs.

The Employees exit quickly, happy to be out of here. Frank alone is left
with a sneaking suspicion...

EXT. FARMERS FIELD - DAY

HIPPY CONCERTGOERS playing hacky-sack, setting up merchandise tables,
laying blankets on the ground.

SUPER: First Day of Festival

INTERVIEW MONTAGE

We meet FIVE YOUNG COLLEGE-AGE GUYS (two wearing "Mt. Tisch University"
shirts). They're not full-on hippies, yet. But getting there. The leader,
JAMES, speaks.

> JAMES
> This is our first fest! We drove twelve hours from Mt.
> Tisch.

> INTERVIEWER (O.S.)
> But that's only three hours away.

                    JAMES
          We stopped to pick dingleberries.

                    OTHER GUY
                (holding out juice)
          To make juice!

Next we see ORTHUR and JEAN APPLE, middle-aged hippies

                    ORTHUR
          We were at the original Woodstock, met there, had kids,
          and stayed.

                    JEAN
          We brought apples and cheese to make wine to use as a
          marinade for our apple/cheese surprise.

Hold on Jean as she considers what she just said.

                    ORTHUR
          Oh...wait...

Then, there's a woman named CHICKEN—

                    CHICKEN
                (frenetic energy)
          I live in a chicken coop, there's no running water or
          heat, and I stopped getting government checks three
          years ago because I broke my ankle doing yoga and I
          sued the United Nations and then Whoopi Goldberg sent
          me a letter. Here.

She holds a tattered letter.

Finally we find an older college-age couple, WAYNE and JANIE.

                    WAYNE
          I'm a grad student, studying Middle Earth Poli-Sci. Just
          wrote a paper on Elves and Trolls, Who Rules the Forest,
          Spells vs. Incantations, etc. And I just need a break. I
          guess I kinda dragged her here.

> JANIE
> Oh it's cool. I like this kind of music. It's all about
> an experience, y'know.

SUPER-WIDE ANGLE SHOT

From high above, a CGI shot of the now-massive audience.

EXT. BACKSTAGE

Oren walks, passing ROADIES and HANGERS-ON. He grins, hits on every chick, grabs drinks and puffs of cigarettes from people's hands and mouths, and takes his share. A nervous Frank follows.

> OREN BURG
> Look at this! All right! Give it to me, what are the
> numbers?

> FRANK
> We totally oversold.

> OREN BURG
> Good.

> FRANK
> We projected four hundred thousand, we've got one
> million, and they're still showing up.

> OREN BURG
> Beautiful.

An ASSISTANT whispers to Frank.

> FRANK
> Oren, one thing, none of the bands are here yet. I mean,
> the show is supposed to start in half an hour.

> OREN BURG
> Yeah, no, I took care of it. Look up . . . here's my boys
> now.

A helicopter lands, or has landed, and the BAND MEMBERS jump out and approach, shouting over the whipping blades.

                         WHEAT
                    (shouting)
               Our helicopter is made entirely of hemp!
                    (beat)
               So's the pilot!

ANGLE ON: Pilot made of hemp.

                                                                  CUT TO:

EXT. ONSTAGE

Oren speaks into a feedbacking mic.

                         OREN BURG
               Okay...people, thank you for coming to Noodlestock!

SFX: Massive applause.

                         OREN BURG (CONT'D)
               We're going to do things a little out of order here.
               Kicking off the festivities will be our headliner, so
               please welcome "The Spaghetti Fish Accident"!

SFX: Supermassive applause.

Oren leaves the stage.

                         WHEAT
               Let's jam!

The song starts. A meandering melody.

                         WHEAT (CONT'D)
               Sugar in the haystack
               feelin' so fine
               Got a bag full of feelin's
               and some cockleberry wine
               Take a bowl of whiskey down to the
               water. Put your honey in an ol' sally
               swing. Drop a bag of lemons in a
               cornball pea patch.
               Tell Old Man Hutch you're gonna love
               everything...

WIDE ANGLE: From the back of the crowd, we see hippy folk enjoying the first strains of this song...and for a moment, all is right with the world.

EXT. BACKSTAGE - CONTINUOUS

Frank and Oren are backstage. Oren is clapping for the band, who glance back at him and smile. Frank is not happy.

> FRANK
> They're the headliners. What's going on?—They don't open the show...

> OREN BURG
> They *are* the show. If they don't open it, who will?

> FRANK
> One of the other twenty-nine bands! I mean, you...
>> (realizing)
> You didn't book anyone else, did you?

Oren smiles, looks back to the band.

> FRANK (CONT'D)
> Shit! Shit!

> OREN BURG
> Enjoy the show, buddy, just enjoy the show.

Oren resumes watching the show, ignoring Frank's rant...

> FRANK
> Dammit! Oren! You flake! I can't...You flakey, greedy...you know you're going to have to pay somebody sometime!

> OREN BURG
>> (scoffing)
> Like who?

> FRANK
> Like the band! You gotta pay them!

                    OREN BURG
Yeah, but I'm charging them two hundred grand to use
that carpet onstage, that's <u>twice</u> what I'm paying them
for the gig.

                    FRANK
Dammit. Well, what about publishing?

                    OREN BURG
Huh?

                    FRANK
Every time they play a song you have to pay publishing
costs!

                    OREN BURG
Fuck! I didn't think about that.

                    FRANK
Aha!

                    OREN BURG
Don't you "aha!" me! Nobody "aha"s me!

Frank scoffs.

                    OREN BURG (CONT'D)
You...all right, yeah...how 'bout this, then?
          (calling to the band onstage)
Keep playin'!

Wheat is confused. Oren does the "stretch" gesture.

                    OREN BURG (CONT'D)
Same song! Keep playin' it! They love it!

Wheat nods, first to Oren, then the band, who kick back into the opening
chords of the same song.

                    FRANK
What the hell?

                    OREN BURG
It's a jam band, that's what people want, anyway.

FRANK
(chuckling)
What? You're gonna have them play one song . . . for three
days?

OREN BURG
Sure. Just give 'em the ol' stretch signal.

Frank is dumbfounded.

OREN BURG (CONT'D)
People used to do it to Hitler all the time, why do you
think he rambled so much?

Oren shouts over the music to the whole band.

OREN BURG (CONT'D)
Same song! Keep playin' the same song! They love it!

Bartholemew, the band member closest to Oren, leans in to get the
lowdown.

OREN BURG (CONT'D)
People are gonna leave if you switch songs on 'em!
They're lovin' it!

Bartholemew nods. Frank storms off. Oren laughs.

MONTAGE

Time Passage, as the band plays "Sugar in the Haystack" all afternoon and
into the evening.

We see The CROWD grooving on it, dancing, taping, smiling.

CUT TO: Our older hippie couple, Orthur and Jean Apple, loving it.

Time passes and The CROWD is less active, some dozing, facing away from
stage, playing hacky-sack.

Land on The five College Kids we met earlier.

COLLEGE KID 2
It's just the same song, man.

> JAMES
> It's all right. It's all right.

> COLLEGE KID 3
> I like the song, but . . . I went to the bathroom and came
> out and it was like déjà vu. Like, how French people
> feel after they shit.

We meet up with Janie and Wayne. Wayne is loving it, Janie is growing
bored, her eyes closing . . .

> WAYNE
> This is a great show. I'm taping it. They love when you
> tape stuff. I think Janie's lovin' it.

> JANIE
> It's weird. I feel, I don't know, like time is . . . being
> wasted.

Now the crowd is bored, staring at the band. Song starts up again, and
offscreen someone shouts.

> SOMEONE (O.S.)
> Noo!

Our camera finds Chicken. She is selling dried peach pits.

> CHICKEN
> Fresh peach pits! Boycott sweatshop sockhops! Peach
> pits, right outta the peach!

EXT. FIELD - NIGHT

The dead of night. Oren sits in a chair reading a paper. He never looks up
as he continues making the "Stretch" sign. The BAND is tired and slouch
against their equipment. Concertgoers sleep in sleeping bags around
them.

EXT. FIELD - DAWN

Hippies rise. We see the band in a further state of exhaustion, still
jamming. The image splits in that outmoded manner, fractured so it can
feature each band member in their own frame, all "lost" in the "jam" . . .
cripes.

ANGLE ON: Frat guys waking...not sure what the noise is. They didn't have a very good sleep.

> COLLEGE KID 2
> Dude, what's that fucking noise?

> COLLEGE KID 3
> It's that band, they're still playing...

ANGLE ON: Orthur and Jean...bright-eyed.

ANGLE ON: Janie and Wayne wake up, having shared a sleeping bag. Wayne feels refreshed.

> WAYNE
> Hey, this is really cool, they're still playing that song!

Janie realizes this is true and is instantly bummed.

> JANIE
> What, really?

> WAYNE
> Yeah...it's really...special.

Wayne grins. Janie shrugs and turns over, and a strange look crosses her face.

EXT. MEDIC TENT

A small medic area under a tarp. Fifteen cots are arranged, most empty, and four MEDICS working.

Pan to a HIPPY GIRL sitting on a cot, staring into space. MEDIC ONE and TWO are waving smelling salts under her nose, checking her pulse, looking into her eyes. Her expression doesn't change. Her WORRIED GIRLFRIEND stands behind her.

> WORRIED GIRLFRIEND
> She didn't drink, she doesn't do drugs, anything...

MEDIC ONE turns to MEDIC TWO.

                  MEDIC ONE
This is the third case I've seen in the last fifteen
minutes . . . something bad is happening.

EXT. BACKSTAGE

Oren is painting on an easel. A painting of a field with a pile of money
in it. Frank rushes in.

                  FRANK
Oren, we got a real problem.

                  OREN BURG
What is it?

                  FRANK
I don't know, some of the kids are comin' down with
something.

                  OREN BURG
It's probably bad acid . . . no! What am I sayin'? This
generation—freaks, probably a bad protein bar.

He laughs it off and walks away . . .

INT. MEDIC TENT

It's getting much busier here. More ZOMBIE KIDS on cots, more standing
about. Most stare off into space. The Medics are hustling but can't
keep up.

                  MEDIC TWO
Oh my God, have you seen the line out there . . . ?

                  MEDIC ONE
Stay cool! It's not a virus, there's no fever . . .

                  MEDIC TWO
But people are drifting off . . . I can't get pulses, their
temperatures are dropping!

                  MEDIC ONE
I know, just think, we'll figure it out—

                    MEDIC TWO
     I can't think! Too many people...and they keep playing
     that damn song—

                    MEDIC ONE
     That's it! That's what it is...they're dying...of
     boredom.

A moment of recognition. Camera pans over to WAYNE wailing.

                    WAYNE
     Janieeeee! Somebody help her!!

Wayne carries Janie's limp body into the tent. Medics rush over, hook her
up to a heart monitor, shoot her with adrenaline.

                    MEDIC ONE
     Get me more adrenaline!

                    MEDIC TWO
     How much do we need?

                    MEDIC ONE
     Whatever you got, call the army, the governor, we need
     to pump these kids full of it...

Medic One grabs Medic Two just before he rushes off.

                    MEDIC ONE (CONT'D)
          (hyperdramatic)
     And tell that band to stop playing that damn song!

Medic One focuses on Janie...

                    MEDIC ONE (CONT'D)
     What's her name?

                    WAYNE
     Janie! I'm a grad student...
          (out of breath, as though it is important)
     I'm a grad student...studying Middle Earth Poli-Sci...
     just wrote a paper on Elves and Trolls...Who Rules the
     Forest, Spells vs. Incantations, etc...a week from this
     Tuesday, I'll find out my grade...

                       MEDIC ONE
            What? So what?

Janie's heart monitor registers flatline.

                 MEDIC ONE (CONT'D)
            No!
                 (to Wayne)
            You idiot! Why'd you waste my time with that story?!!

                       WAYNE
            ...It's not really a story...it's just...

Medic One works furiously to save Janie.

SFX: Heart Monitor, flatline sound.

Medic One covers Janie's face with a sheet before moving on to another
victim.

                  WAYNE (CONT'D)
          What? What happened?
              (falling to his knees)
          Noooooo!!!!

This word transitions us to...

                                         DISSOLVE TO:

EXT. SUPER-DUPER MULTIPLEX

                     DROOPY
          Noooooooo...nope...

A VERY ANNOYED BOX OFFICE ATTENDANT stands in front of a massive marquee
advertising thirty-six movies and starting times. She stares at a guy who
is trying to pick one to see...it's DROOPY.

                  DROOPY (CONT'D)
          No...not that one...not that one either...

                    ATTENDANT
                (sternly)
        What movie do you want to see, sir? There are other
        people in line.

                    DROOPY
        I don't know. I'd like to see...a movieeeee...
        that's a...comedyyyyyy...with some dramaaaa—action-
        eyyyyy...

DOLLY DOWN a line of annoyed MOVIE NERDS, some sitting in camping
chairs under a shade umbrella. LAND ON Bob and David at the end of the
line.

                    BOB
        David, check out this line.

                    DAVID
        Yeah, this must be a blockbuster.

David taps the shoulder of HARRY, a MOVIE NERD sitting in a folding chair ahead of him. Harry shares a cooler with his friend, DREW.

> DAVID (CONT'D)
> Excuse me, guys, what film are you in line for?

> HARRY
> It's gonna be awesome!

> DAVID
> No, I asked you which movie are you waiting in line for?

Harry looks at Drew, Drew shrugs.

> DREW
> The new one.

> BOB
> But you don't know which one it is?

> HARRY
> Nope. I bet we like it, though.

> DREW
> Yup.

They high-five.

> BOB
> So, you're fans of movies . . . in general.

They nod.

CUT BACK TO:

EXT. HOLLYWOOD BLVD

The front of the line.

> DROOPY
> . . . can I just buy one ticket and sneak into every theatre?

                        ATTENDANT
No.

                        DROOPY
Okay. What's the best movie you have?

                        ATTENDANT
My boss says I'm not supposed to recommend movies.

                        DROOPY
Well, if you don't like movies, why do you work here?
        (laughs to himself)

                        ATTENDANT
        (groans)

                        DROOPY
        (celebrating—to no one)
That shut her up!

                        ATTENDANT
I like movies! So do all the people in line behind you.
They'd like to see one, this week.

                        DROOPY
Uhhh...okay...

ANGLE ON: Bob and David talking to the movie nerds.

                        DREW
We see every movie the day it comes out.

                        HARRY
At least once.

                        DAVID
But what if it sucks?

Harry and Drew are taken aback by this suggestion.

                        HARRY
        (defensive)
It's gonna be great.

                    DAVID
          Maybe, but what if it sucks?

                    DREW
          It's gonna be totally awesome.

                    BOB
          How do you know that? You don't even know what it is?!

A beat.

                    DREW
          Well, look at the line.

Others in line agree.

                    OTHER NERDS
          Yeah / It's really long...

Bob and David shake their heads.

SFX: Kooky car horn which plays snippet of "Hooray for Hollywood."

Bob and David turn to see an old timey Model-T car drive by, festooned
with colorful crepe and balloons, a sign on the side reading "The Mayor
Of Hollywood." In the front is a CHAUFFEUR. In the back seat the MAYOR
sits, waving to passersby (we recognize him from the painting in the DMV
office break room).

                    BOB
          The Mayor of Hollywood!

                    DAVID
          Great. And we've got just fifteen minutes left!

EXT. OFFICE DOOR

Sign on the frosted glass door reads, "The Mayor of Hollywood."

Bob and David enter.

                                              DISSOLVE TO:

INT. MAYOR'S OFFICE

Dolly across various movie memorabilia and posters: *Attack of the Machines!* (featuring typewriters, large calculators, with legs), *She-Apes of the Amazon*, a full-sized stuffed bear holding a gun beside a poster of *Bears with Guns!* and *Vampire Darkie—Double the Trouble!* The poster features a young, black, "hip" vampire.

                    BOB (O.S.)
          Wow...some real ancient artifacts.

                    DAVID (O.S.)
          Yeah...I bet this stuff is worth a lot...to weirdos.

                    BOB (O.S.)
          Yeah.

Suddenly, a door opens. The Mayor steps out of his private bathroom, the toilet flushing behind him.

                    THE MAYOR
          Whoo!
               (re: his turd)
          Talk about the birth of a nation...

The Mayor shuffles over to his desk. He has a riding crop and wears jodhpurs, argyle cardigan, etc.

                    BOB
          Mr. Mayor.

                    DAVID
          Hi, we're Bob and David. We just need your signature.

David shows the Mayor the slip from Carlotta.

                    THE MAYOR
          I used to be king of the movies!

                    BOB
          That's great.

David checks the clock...it's broken and covered in dust.

                    DAVID
But if you could just sign this—we're trying to make our
own movie.

                    THE MAYOR
What's your gimmick?

                    DAVID
Huh?

                    THE MAYOR
Your gimmick, kid. How you gonna reel 'em in? All my
movies had a gimmick.
          (points to a poster)
Attack of the Machines, we threw wires at the audience,
scared 'em half to death.
          (another poster)
Day of the Man with the One Arm That Was Like a Crab's!
When it played we would throw live crabs on 'em. People
loved it!

                    BOB
Okay, well, we thought we'd have the theatre sell
popcorn and drinks.

                    THE MAYOR
Wild! Won't work, though, already tried it.

He points to a poster for *Popcorn Monster Returns!*

                    THE MAYOR (CONT'D)
People don't like popcorn at the movies. Too delicious.

                    DAVID
          (pointing to a poster)
What's that one?

We see the poster for *One-Eyed Aliens of Planet Mars!* This is the most
normal-looking poster of all; horrified faces in the foreground, a typical
'50s spaceship opening its hatch, barely revealing the shadow of the
Alien.

                    THE MAYOR
          (ruefully)

That was the movie that ruined me. Scared the entire
nation. Did well in Europe, though.

                    BOB
Great. Now, if you could just sign...

                    THE MAYOR
Watch! And learn...

He starts the film projector on his desk and we see:

(*NOTE* This is a low budget sci-fi movie trailer ala *Plan Nine from Outer
Space*.)

MUSIC: "Scary" theremin, organ sci-fi theme

Shot of twinkling stars (a black cloth with pinholes and light behind it).

                    ANNOUNCER (V.O.)
                (bombastic)
Look! Into the sky! Behind the cloth of night, do you
see the hundreds of beautiful twinkling stars? But wait!
What would you do if there suddenly appeared...

Title Card wipes onscreen...

                    ANNOUNCER (V.O.)
        One-Eyed Aliens of Planet Mars!

                                                    CUT TO:

EXT. SUBURBAN STREET

MUSIC: Sweet, innocent melody

DENNIS MCBOY, a typical '50s movie ten-year-old, plays jacks on the
sidewalk.

                    DENNIS
                (sing-songy)
La, la, loo, Jacksaroo, tell the king he's eating stew.

                    ANNOUNCER (V.O.)
How will you feel when...

The music rises in pitch as a shadow crosses the sidewalk.

> ANNOUNCER (V.O.)
> ...visitors from outer space appear?!

Dennis looks up, the shadow crosses his face, he runs, leaving his jacks behind.

CUT TO:

INT. EFFECT SHOT

A typical cheapo pie-plate-on-a-string type of flying saucer hovers and lands next to a model of the White House.

INT. WHITE HOUSE

The PRESIDENT speaks directly to camera, as on a TV news special report.

> PRESIDENT
> Citizens of America, it is I, your President. Alien
> super-beings from Mars have landed here in Washington.
> Do not be afraid. General Rutgers...

BRIEF ANGLE ON: GENERAL RUTGERS, '50s crewcut general, standing behind President.

> PRESIDENT (CONT'D)
> ...of the US Armed Forces has spoken to them on the
> wireless radio and assures me that they come in peace
> with many wondrous things to teach us.

> ANNOUNCER (V.O.)
> How will our leaders react to the unscheduled arrival of
> strange visitors from beyond?

CUT TO:

EXT. WHITE HOUSE LAWN

The PRESIDENT and GENERAL RUTGERS stand on a platform beside a cheapo cardboard spaceship. Other world leaders are there: CHINESE MAO GUY, SAUDI PRINCE FELLA. The President checks his watch, the general shrugs.

CUT TO:

EXT. SAME

                    ANNOUNCER (V.O.)
          What about regular people?

White-bread CITIZENS, including little DENNIS, stand behind army lines,
anxious and excited. A SCARED YOUNG SOLDIER holding a rifle stands in
front of them.

EXT. WHITE HOUSE

ANGLE ON: Rocket ship.

SFX: Cheapo futuristic door opening on spacecraft!

MUSIC: Tension rising

CUTAWAYS TO:

Nervous CITIZENS assembled.

INT. BAR - NERVOUS BUSINESSMEN and some DRUNKS, watching it on TV.

> ANNOUNCER (V.O.)
> How about Swedish folks?!—

A FAMILY in a SWEDISH HOME, also watching on TV.

The tension rises—the door opens, smoke billows—

The CAMERA PANS up the body of the aliens; they have three toes, but otherwise have relatively normal bodies, and they're wearing silvery space suits. Before we see their heads, we CUT AWAY to...

> ANNOUNCER (V.O.)
> And how will _you_ react when you see—

CITIZENS squinting, jaws dropping, covering their children's faces.

The WORLD LEADERS, appalled.

We hear the aliens speak—

> ALIEN #2 (O.S.)
> (in corny '50s alien voice)
> Greetings. We come in peace.

ANGLE ON: Speechless President and General.

As MUSIC CRESCENDOES.

ANGLE ON: Alien's head, it is shaped like a giant penis.

> ANNOUNCER (V.O.)
> _One-Eyed Aliens of Planet Mars!_

Title GRAPHIC wipes frame, then drops out as another Alien with penis head enters the shot.

> ANNOUNCER (V.O.)
> See our leaders get flustered!

ANGLE ON: The President.

> PRESIDENT
> Oh my God, they look like my penis!

Off the GENERAL'S shocked reaction.

> PRESIDENT (CONT'D)
> I mean, well, anyone's penis...you know what I mean...
> I'm nervous...

ANGLE ON: ALIEN #2.

> ALIEN #2
> We come bearing tidings of peace and great benefit for
> all Earth people!

> ALIEN #1
> Let's all hug and jump around!

> ANNOUNCER (V.O.)
> See Americans in panic!

INT. AMERICAN FAMILY HOME

Pipe-smoking DAD and MOM grab kids and hustle them along.

                    DAD
          Kids, hurry! Into the bomb shelter!

INT. BAR

Guys in the bar raise a ruckus, while others faint.

                                              CUT TO:

INT. SWEDISH FAMILY HOME

                    ANNOUNCER (V.O.)
          See Europeans reacting maturely!

The Swedish family watches the penis-alien cavorting on-screen. They are
unmoved. (They speak in Swedish with subtitles.)

                    SWEDISH DAD
          Interesting. Do you like it, kids?

                    SWEDISH KIDS
          Ya. I like the aliens.

                    SWEDISH MOM
          Let's see what else is on.

The Swedish Dad switches the channel and they watch some people having
sex. Again, the family is unmoved, enjoying the show.

EXT. WHITE HOUSE

Chaos.

ANGLE ON: The Scared Soldier levels his machine gun at the Aliens, and
fires. Mayhem ensues. The World Leaders run amok.

Behind him, Dennis shouts—

                         DENNIS
              Duck, Mr. Alien, duck!

The spaceship door closes, leaving Alien #1 stranded outside, dodging
bullets.

Dennis heads towards the Alien. The Alien, confused and frightened, tries
to save Dennis from the bullets, picking him up. The General thinks the
Alien is kidnapping the boy—

                         GENERAL
              Fire at will!

Alien #1 and Dennis run away, into the woods.

                                                              CUT TO:

EXT. SUBURBAN STREET AT DUSK

We see the Alien carrying Dennis, ducking behind hedges. A police car
races by, sirens a-wailing.

                    RADIO NEWS (O.C.)
              Once again, a heightened state of alert has been issued
              by the President. Be on the lookout for the alien. It
              is approximately seven feet tall and looks like the
              President's penis. Well, anyone's penis, really...

INT. DENNIS'S BEDROOM

Typical cowboy bedspread and wallpaper. The ALIEN and Dennis sit on the
bed listening to the transistor radio.

                    RADIO NEWS(O.C.)
              ...If you're a man, I mean. Anyway, you can't miss it.
              Penis is the key word here.

Dennis switches the radio off.

                         DENNIS
              I don't get it, Mr. Alien, why is everyone so mad at you?

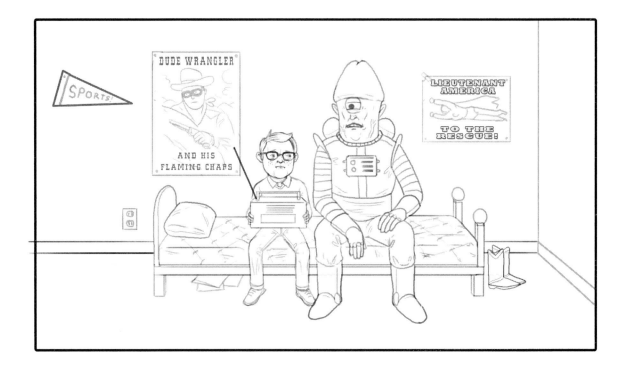

The Alien takes Dennis's hand.

> ALIEN
> I don't know, Denny. If only humans were more like you.
> I cannot believe that I will never again see my penis-
> shaped son Chloron. You'd like him, Dennis, he's a lot
> like you, but shaped like a penis.

They hug. A single tear drips from the Alien's one eye.

> DENNIS
> It's okay, you'll be safe. My dad's a good guy, he'll
> figure out a way to help you.

> ANNOUNCER (V.O.)
> Can a one-eyed Alien from the planet Mars really live
> amongst us?

EXT. MCBOY HOUSE

Dennis's Dad and the Alien exit the house dressed in business suits, carrying
pipes and briefcases. Mom and Dennis wave good-bye to the two "men."

INT. SUBURBAN HOUSE.

A young COUPLE sit on a couch, listening to the Alien's sales pitch. The Alien is still wearing a fedora.

> ALIEN
> And with our premium deductible for Mom you'll save over ten percent.

> WIFE
> That sounds like an A-Number-One deal.

> HUSBAND
> We'll take it.

He shakes hands with the Alien, who smiles.

> WIFE
> Are you sure we can't take your hat for you?

> ALIEN
> Oh, thank you, my first sale, how exciting...

The YOUNG COUPLE grin, but then get a look of worry on their faces as though something is coming at them...

                                               CUT BACK TO:

Graphic accompanies the following announcement.

> ANNOUNCER (V.O.)
> See *One-Eyed Aliens of Planet Mars* filmed in Splash-O-Vision!

INT. MOVIE THEATRE

A '50s MOVIE AUDIENCE watching this very movie, smiling, really into it...get splashed with white viscous liquid and react, with more disgust than fear.

> AUDIENCE MEMBER
> What the hell?

                    AUDIENCE MEMBER #2
          Eeewwww! It's salty!

The film clip ends, and we are back in the—

INT. MAYOR'S OFFICE

Bob and David can't believe what they have seen.

                    BOB
          So, that didn't work, huh?

                    THE MAYOR
          Well, yes and no. It scared people...but in the wrong
          way. Anyway, here's your paper.

                    DAVID
          Oh, shit, Bob, it's five to five!

Bob and David tear out the door.

                    THE MAYOR
          Best of luck...

The door slams on his last word...

EXT. HOLLYWOOD BLVD - DUSK, AND I MEAN IT

MUSIC: SCORED FOR DRAMATIC EMPHASIS till the end...

Bob and David are running down the street, checking their watches.

                    BOB
          Great, we got everything. But we might be too late...

                    DAVID
          Don't worry, Bob, she'll keep it open for us.

                                                      CUT TO:

EXT. STREET

Metal gate closing. CARLOTTA is locking up, muttering good-bye to one
other EMPLOYEE.

>   CARLOTTA
>   Bye, Dwayne, see ya tomorrow.

Bob and David come running up.

>   BOB
>   What's going on?

>   DAVID
>   It's not five o'clock yet. There's still a minute.

>   CARLOTTA
>   Not by my watch, honey.

>   DAVID
>   But we've got everything.

>   BOB
>   Please.

Carlotta sighs.

>   CARLOTTA
>   Show me what you got.

She "Mm-hmms" through the following...

>   BOB
>   Well, here's our physicals. We're in great shape.

>   DAVID
>   Here's the lock of hair from the producer. It's a little
>   greasy.

>   BOB
>   Here's our concept. We wrote it down on this napkin.

>   DAVID
>   Oh, and here's our blue slip, signed by the Mayor of
>   Hollywood.

          CARLOTTA
Well...mm-hm, "a twenty-dollar hot dog!"
    (chuckles)
...Okay, well, it looks like everything is in order.

ANGLE ON: Bob and David, excited. Carlotta is about to stamp it, but—

          CARLOTTA (CONT'D)
Wait a second, you don't have a star.

          BOB
What?

          CARLOTTA
You have to have a star attached honey, to star in your
film.

          DAVID
What about us?

          CARLOTTA
I'm sorry. I don't think so. Oh, well. Best of luck.

She heads off down the street leaving Bob and David standing there,
forlorn. Rain begins to fall on them.

          BOB
Damn.

          DAVID
Well, I guess I'd better get my shining mittens.

          BOB
And sauce...

          DAVID
All because we couldn't get a star.

          BOB
Yeah...

Bob looks up. A hint of awareness in his eye.

                                    BOB (CONT'D)
                        Wait a second, David...

ANGLE: Over the shoulders of Bob and David we see Carlotta waddling away,
carrying her overloaded shopping bag.

                                    BOB (CONT'D)
                        ...I got an idea.

MUSIC: Sting

ANGLE ON: David grins...he gets it, too.

                                                            DIP TO BLACK:

(NOTE: THE NEXT PIECE IS A MOVIE TRAILER WITHIN A TRAILER. IT'S A BIT
COMPLEX, WITH TWO ANNOUNCERS WHO OVERLAP A BIT.)

BLOCKBUSTER TRAILER

Over black—

                                    ANNOUNCER ONE (V.O.)
                        In a world of blockbuster movies...

GRAPHIC: From the center of the screen come the words "In a world turned
upside down." simultaneous with ANNOUNCER #2—

                                    ANNOUNCER TWO (V.O.)
                        In a world turned upside down.

                                                            CUT TO:

EXT. NEW YORK PANORAMA

SFX: Massive rumble.

The image of New York shudders and flips.

                                    ANNOUNCER ONE (V.O.)
                        Where the latest big movie is a must-see...

As the dust settles on the upside-down New York, another graphic comes at
us from center-screen.

GRAPHIC: "This one's a must-see . . . Clyve Dailey, *The Beaver-Bop Report*"

                    ANNOUNCER TWO (V.O.)
              Where everything is topsy-turvy . . .

                                                    CUT TO:

INT. APARTMENT BEDROOM

(NOTE: This next scene is shot upside down. In a real room, we anchor the actors to the ceiling, and when they "stand" they are standing upside down, with their hair hanging down, and coins falling out of their pockets. HOWEVER, the camera is also flipped, so it appears they are standing up . . . but not really—)

DAVID is a futuristic guy, with a crazy tattoo on his neck, and wakes up next to TRINA, a tough hottie (think Franka Potente). He looks around and notices the CHANDELIER next to him, on the ceiling.

                         DAVID
              Goddammit . . . no!

Trina sits up.

                         TRINA
              What is it, Dex?

                         DAVID
              Every day this city is upside down I think "This
              nightmare has to end!" and every damn morning I wake up
              from the nightmare, which I'm still in!

She hugs him.

                         TRINA
              Be quiet, Dex! The Gravity Meister will hear you.

A knock on the door. Bob opens it. He enters wearing heavy boots, carrying a large plastic jug. His hair is rock-and-roll long, he's got a leather vest, and he speaks with a British accent like the drug dealer in *Withnail and I*.

                         BOB
              —do I 'ear some little birds calling my name?

David and Trina recoil.

                    BOB (CONT'D)
                (shaking his juice)
            Does someone need a slug of gravity juice to settle
            their equilibrium?

                    DAVID
                (desperate)
            I do. Please.

                    BOB
            Catch then, little fella—

Bob tosses the jug and it flies up...which is really down, which makes no
sense, of course.

                    ANNOUNCER ONE (V.O.)
            And the story is a train wreck of clichés—

                                                    CUT TO:

INT. BEDROOM

Close on David trying to drink the juice from the container, it spills all over his forehead, as he is upside down.

                      ANNOUNCER TWO (V.O.)
           One man fights to make it right.

EXT. MOVIE THEATRE

Bob, as the Gravity Meister, David as Dex, fight with swords in front of this movie theatre.

SFX: Massive, overdone "swooshing" noises.

As the fight continues, we PULL OUT...

REVEAL the above trailer is being watched on a mobile monitor, the kind they put outside theatres to advertise. A mob of our movie nerds from the prior scenes stand around the monitor, loving it.

                      ANNOUNCER ONE (V.O.)
         Two men refuse to go along with the herd.

Actors portraying Harry and Drew are in the mob.

                      HARRY
               It's awesome!

                      DREW
         I've seen it twice!—today!

ANGLE ON: Bob and David, as themselves, watching the above trailer in the street.

                      BOB
        I don't know, I don't get it.

                      HARRY
         What's not to get?

                      DAVID
        Yeah, I just don't think I'd like it.

                        DREW
            What's not to think to like?!

Harry and Drew and the MOB OF NERDS stare at them, confounded.

CLOSE-UPS, Dramatic moves.

Bob and David back away.

                        BOB
            Uh...come on David, let's get out of here.

                    ANNOUNCER ONE (V.O.)
            Even friends and family turn on them...

EXT. STABLES

David and Bob pass a camel stable. Camera DOLLIES BACK to include other
STABLE WORKERS on lunch break, eyeing them suspiciously.

                        JULIA
            He hasn't even seen it once!

                        OSWALD
            Neither of them has seen it!

ZOOM IN on EMILIO, tight Dutch angle close-up!

                        EMILIO
            I'll kill them! I'll kill them, then I'll take their
            eyeballs and put them into my pockets and go to the
            movie, <u>then</u> they will see the goddamn movie!

                    ANNOUNCER ONE (V.O.)
            Rejected by all, unable to find a single kindred
            soul...

INT. BAR - NIGHT

BOB is talking to a GIRL.

                        GIRL
            It's just like in the movie, y'know, the scene on the
            edge of the planet?

BOB is confused.

> GIRL (CONT'D)
> You know, where New York is upside down. Because of the
> moons and the nuclear war?

Bob shrugs.

> GIRL (CONT'D)
> You're an idiot.

> ANNOUNCER ONE (V.O.)
> ...even family members...

EXT. BACKYARD BARBECUE

David is there with his MOM, DAD, SISTER, and her HUSBAND and KID. The
KID (10) wears a shirt that says "New York, York New," weird heavy ski-
type boots, and swings a sword.

> KID
> Look at me! I'm on the ceiling!

Everyone laughs. David laughs. Everyone stops laughing and shoots angry
looks at David.

> DAD
> What the hell are you laughing at? You haven't seen it.

> DAVID'S MOM
> See the movie, son.

> DAVID'S SISTER
> See it.

> DAVID'S BROTHER-IN-LAW
> See the damn thing!

David fights back tears and backs away...

> ANNOUNCER ONE (V.O.)
> Two renegades are forced to walk the earth...

CUT TO:

EXT. FOREST - DAY

BOB AND DAVID, hungry and cold, walk through the rain, nibbling on pieces of bread.

> ANNOUNCER (V.O.)
> ...and live by their wits on the outskirts of civilization.

CUT TO:

EXT. FOREST

Bob and David looking haggard, sitting by a campfire.

> DAVID
> Got any more of that gum?

> BOB
> I'm fryin' up the last piece.

A stick of gum is hanging off a spit over the campfire.

EXT. STICK LEAN-TO - NIGHT

We are high in the Georgian Mountains (Russia). Bob and David walk over a ridge.

> ANNOUNCER (V.O.)
> Until finally, they find one woman with the sass to set them straight.

They stop walking, both love struck by what they see.

ANGLE ON: Lean-to, there is a small fire, and chickens running about.

Out of the front comes CARLOTTA, in raggedy clothes. She chases the chickens.

> CARLOTTA
> You get over here, you ragamuffins, tell Carlotta your troubles.

Bob and David run toward her, slo-mo.

MUSIC: Romantic

> ANNOUNCER (V.O.)
> It's a story of love and redemption, featuring a song
> that you just can't get out of your head.

EXT. LEAN-TO

Bob and David dance raucously with Carlotta to what sounds like Motown.

> FAKE MOTOWN SONG
> ...Get it...get it...gonna get it, girl, and give it
> right back to you...

> ANNOUNCER (V.O.)
> ...and ending with a surprise that you have to see to
> believe...check it out—

                                                      CUT TO:

EXT. SAME, OUTSIDE THE LEAN-TO

Bob, David, and Carlotta collect sticks to make something.

EXT. SAME, OUTSIDE THE LEAN-TO

They have built a rocket ship out of sticks. Bob, David, and Carlotta are
preparing to fly away.

> BOB
> Off we go.

> DAVID
> To a better world. Where we won't have to see that
> movie.

> BOB
> Or any movie.

> CARLOTTA
> Don't you say that! Don't you ever say that!

                         BOB
          I'm sorry.

David lights a long fuse on the spaceship, then the three of them jump in,
and Bob closes the door.

SFX: Rocket sounds.

EXT. EARTH

Footage of Earth from above.

                         ANNOUNCER (V.O.)
          Follow them as they travel through the stars to find a
          planet of their own.

INT. ROCKET SHIP

Bob and David working various controls. Setting dials. Carlotta happily
eating cookies.

The rocket ship lands, shaking about wildly, but then, calm.

EXT. ROCKET SHIP

Smoke billows about. The door opens. Bob steps out, weary from the trip.
David follows. Then Carlotta. They grin to see the sun, breathe deeply.

POV ANGLE: Smoke fills their eyes, but as it clears they see they are on
Earth. On Hollywood Blvd., to be precise. Directly in front of the line of
moviegoers who originally wanted their heads.

ANGLE ON: Bob, David, Carlotta, shocked.

                         BOB
          Oh, shit.

ANGLE ON: Harry and Drew, and other NERDS.

                    HARRY
          It's them! Get 'em!

The nerds descend on our guys, swarming with ill-intentions.

Camera CRANES UP over this mob scene.

MUSIC: Triumphant

> ANNOUNCER (V.O.)
> *Blockbuster Movie*...coming this fall!

When the music ends, we hear a director shout...

> DIRECTOR
> Cut! Print! That was great! We got it!

The CRANE SHOT LOOSENS, and we can see the mob of looky-loos who stopped to see the filming of this final shot. Amongst them are Bob and David, exactly where they were at the beginning of the film.

They turn and head off, and we hear their dialogue over their backs as they disappear...

                    BOB
          Wow, David, huh?

                    DAVID
          Yeah, Bob, movie magic!

                    BOB
              (looking around)
          Where?!

                    DAVID
          Right there, what we just saw.

                    BOB
          Oh. Yeah.

THE END

Some Reminiscences,
Just for You!

Here are some notes on the pieces in *Bob and David Make a Movie,* straight from the recollections of the fading memories of Bob and David and Brian:

HOLLYWOOD TOWN HALL (pp. 8–18)

FYI: We know there are aspiring filmmakers who will be reading this, but we have to make it clear that there is no place to go to APPLY for a movie. Trust us, we looked everywhere. If it were only this easy. Instead of a nasty, bureaucratic, DMV-type building where you wait in line to justify your creative vision to a sassy black woman (remember the Pine-Sol spokeslady?), in Hollywood it is absolutely necessary to be courteous and spend YEARS feigning interest and respect for a cabal of slippery, contemptible, arguably evil douchebags and douchebag-ettes. Now you know…go buy that bus ticket and get out here!

KOREAN MOVIE RIPOFFS (pp. 18–27)

In New York you can buy bootlegs of any movie right on the street. Sometimes they're okay, sometimes they're shitty versions filmed by people in a movie theatre. David notes, "When I was in China, for a dollar you could get DVDs of major Hollywood movies that were just out or just about to come out…because that's where they make the actual DVDs. Literally, only a dollar for the latest American films." To which Bob asks, "When were you in China? They didn't make a chipmunk movie there, did they?" To which David replies: "Yes they did, it's called *Chip-Fucked* and I'm in it and I have a thirteen-inch cock and a nine-inch pussy, so F.U.!" Which makes Bob sneeze into his silk handkerchief. It also makes Brian throw up on his erection.

HOLLYWOOD DOCTOR (pp. 27–32)

This character is based on all of our agents. Agents are fast talkers, big planners, and often have extremely short attention spans. They impatiently pretend to listen to you as you spout your meaningless (to them) career goals, then the second you stop to inhale, they push you to do whatever it is that's just come across their desk. "Yeah, yeah, I hear you, you've got a script about your teen traumas that you've nurtured for a while, we'll get to that in a minute… Right now I want to hear you tell me how much you want to write a film version of the book *Everyone Poops*. We just got the rights! Kids love it, it doesn't have to have talking poo in it, but…maybe the butthole is talking, I'm not the writer, this is your job, but I would say if the butthole talks then you got Jake Gyllenhaal, who I happen to rep, and he's wanted to portray an animated sphincter for a while now! Let me get Jake on the phone—Tanya, get JG."

Brian shares this story… "One of the only times I had a phone call when I was signed with a big agent for three weeks he asked, 'What do you want to do?' I said, 'I'd be open to a meeting at *SNL*, I wouldn't be happy there, but…' He interrupted me, shouting across the room, 'Tanya! Get Lorne Michaels on the phone!' Nothing came of it. I was not surprised."

DOUBLE DATE (LETHA BOMBZ) (pp. 33–37)

There's the solid couple and there's the guy who's always got a new girlfriend and you have to keep meeting them and acting happy when you can smell another breakup around the corner. But, really, David also never dated anybody that bimbo-ish. David replies, "Well you don't really *date* bimbos. It's not necessary." But this isn't a fully realized sketch. It's more of a link to the "Strippertown" sketch, which *is* a fully realized sketch.

STRIPPERTOWN (pp. 37–48)

"Strippertown" was Brian Posehn's idea. Brian likes to brag, "Strippers sometimes act like they're your girlfriend, and the idea for the sketch came from an idiot buying into that. At the time we were writing this I went to strip clubs pretty frequently, both in the Valley and when I was on the road. My shitty logic was: it's not cheating if I PAY for a girl to rub my dick. Real girls hitting on me at the time freaked me out. But strippers weren't the same because you know they don't really like you and a lot of them are robots." He goes on to share this terribly sad story of broken humans interacting: "There was one stripper in Atlanta that was extra nice and fake-girlfriendy. When I revisited the strip club several months later a different stripper came up to me and told me, 'You broke Fake Name's heart' because I'd told this previous stripper I was going to come back and I didn't…for a while. This scene is just taking that idea, in the *Mr. Show* way, to its ridiculous extreme."

HOLLYWOOD TELEPHONE (pp. 48–55)

It's true that when you go out to eat in Hollywood you are surrounded by people pitching movies loudly, talking about projects they're shooting, wanting to shoot, and just finished shooting, also loudly. You can't really help overhearing the ideas, and this can be very entertaining and pathetic. One time David and Bob were in a restaurant and two producers were loudly discussing a road movie that was going to be so fun and so cheap to make and one of them burst out, "I can get Puck!" Puck, being the one-time bad-boy reality show celebrity from MTV's *The Real World: San Francisco*. Not an actor, but we still hope that movie got made.

RAGING RACERS (pp. 55–71)

This is a fever dream based on the film *Moulin Rouge* and how "gay-tastic" it was—with the maudlin, overly dramatic singing and all the flouncing around. Here we are using "gay" in the immature fourteen-year-old homophobe sense of the word. But then, really, the sketch is about a bunch of young guys being afraid to call the movie "gay" because they are trying to be politically correct. But, in the course of doing so, they are not being honest.

This is the kind of scene that leans on performance and would become three times as funny in execution—with all the room for overcooked performances, silly riffs, and a lot of fun to be found in editing. David imagineers a shot: "Camera goes in to somebody's eyeball and out their asshole and then the lens has slight brown tinge in all its corners for the rest of the sequence." Nice, David. Thank you for that.

ROBOT STREET PERFORMER (pp. 71–75)

Brian Posehn would play the street performer. He is the last person who should try to be a street performer. "I was a curmudgeon at twenty-two," he proudly states. Not being a people person, he is also able to sound incredibly sarcastic while merely being straightforward. Also, for inspiration, we all hate street performers.

NOODLEFEST (pp. 75–96)

This marries our hatred of jam bands with our detestation of sleazy Hollywood producers. People in Hollywood are often trying to save money by simply insisting that "no one will notice" the lack of quality/effort/production. In a weird way, the audiences of jam bands really would be willing to put up with a never-ending song and would feel obliged to be proud of it as well…once you get past the normal pop length of three minutes, who's to say how long a good song should be?

MULTIPLEX NERDS (pp. 96–100)

These nerds are our friends, we know these people, we are (Brian *is*) these people. Respect!

MAYOR OF HOLLYWOOD (pp. 100–103)

We were dreaming of Dan Aykroyd for this. Once again, it addresses how hard it is to get a movie made and the scrambling effort to make a project work by giving it a hook!

ONE-EYED ALIENS (pp. 103–112)

Well, this one is a doozy of a gem and a real sweetheart to boot! A *Mr. Show*-ish scene, with a point of view about Americans and their relationship to sex.

Certainly Americans of the '50s and '60s. David: "Please take note we play it smart and restrained through most of the sketch and then, only at the end, do we blow our load."

BLOCKBUSTER MOVIE (pp. 115–126)

This is about the social pressure to go see the latest huge-ass Hollywood mega-mess. Sometimes you find yourself thinking, "I really *should* see *Avatar*, or I won't be able to talk to anyone ever again, I won't understand what anyone's talking about, and I'll never win another trivia contest in my life." None of us saw and we still haven't seen *Titanic*, so you can understand how lonely (and supercool) we are.

HOORAY FOR AMERICA!

by Bob Odenkirk and David Cross

First Draft on March 17th, 1998

OPEN ON: THIS PARAGRAPH ON-SCREEN:

"The following is a work of fiction. Current U.S. election laws make it impossible for any single corporation to 'buy' the Presidency."

DIP TO BLACK, THEN UP ON:

"However, we're working on it."

BURN IN *GLOBO-CHEM* LOGO; A SPINNING GLOBE

                    ANNOUNCER (V.O.)
          A message from your friends at Globo-Chem and the Globo-
          Chem family of companies. Makers of everything from...

For each item he names, we see a picture of the product which is listed in the accompanying parenthetical—

                    ANNOUNCER (V.O.)
          Farm Supplies...
               (guy on tractor)
          To the bread you eat...
               (suburban kitchen, kid eating sandwich, Mom smiling)
          Surgical lasers...
               (patient having a sex change with a laser)
          Popcorn substitutes...
               (couple in theatre eating something weird)
          Sewage treatment...
               (large sewage treatment plant)
          Sewage...
               (sewage)
          Rabbits...
               (rabbits)
          Relationship helpers...
               (man modeling bondage gear for his mate)
          Cancer research...
               (scientists working on "poison foam"—this will matter
               later in the story)
          From rock-n-roll posters...
               (poster of a rock band)
          To leisure wear...

(a sweatshop in China)
Globo-Chem fills your world with things.

An animated PIT PAT pops up in the lower corner and waves

                    ANNOUNCER (V.O.)
          Wherever you see Pit Pat you know you are part of a
          wonderful worldwide corporation.

                    PIT PAT
          Take it from me—I LOVE you!

And a final sting that is suddenly somewhat ominous.

                    ANNOUNCER (V.O.)
          Globo-Chem—"**A better world for better people.**"

                                        DIP TO BLACK AND UP ON:

INT. BACKSTAGE

We are in a small, ramshackle backstage area. Mirrors with lots of
burned-out bulbs around them.

MUSIC: In the background is preshow circusy music

Bob and David are warming up for a show. Bob is dressed in a flashy,
furry, red, white, and blue, '70s pimp outfit. David is wearing a foam map
of America. His hat is Alaska and his feet are Hawaii. Bob does a vocal
warm-up . . .

                    BOB
          I never knew that naughty Nettie nicked her knickers
          from Nelson Eddy. I never knew that naughty Nettie . . .

David peeks through a hole in the wall at the audience.

                    DAVID
          It's fillin' up.

They high-five.

                    DAVID (CONT'D)
          Hey, we're doing great, man.

                    BOB
Hey, David, we're going all the way, right?

                    DAVID
To Mars?

                    BOB
No, come on.

                    DAVID
Oh, yeah, to the top.

                    BOB
Right. Which part of the top?

                    DAVID
The tip.

                    BOB
The tip-top of the...

David is confused, feeling pressure...

                    BOB (CONT'D)
...of the mip-mop! Come on!

                    DAVID
          (immediately)
Mip-mop! The tip-top of the mip-mop! God, I wish there
was a way I could remember that...

                    BOB
It's simple, just remember TTOTMM—"The Tired Otter
Taunts Marilyn Monster"...simple.

                    DAVID
Right, thanks.

Bob pulls out his phone.

                    BOB
Cool. I'm just so excited, I've got to call them again.
          (into phone)
Oh, hey, Mom, it's Bob.

                    MOM (V.O.)
          Bobby, is that you?

                    BOB
          Listen...

Bob holds the receiver up to the hole in the wall, picking up the sound of
the mingling audience in the theatre.

                    BOB (CONT'D)
          Hear that? That's a crowd. They came to see me, in a
          real show.

                    MOM (V.O.)
          Well, I don't know. Here's your father.

Briefly, Bob listens to his Mom and Dad having an argument in their
living room somewhere. Bob shrugs to David, who is shaving his legs with
a straight razor. Finally, Bob's Dad gets on the line: his always-angry
voice bursting through—

                    DAD (V.O.)
          What?

                    BOB
          Dad! Hey, I'm in show business. I've made it!

                    DAD (V.O.)
          You ain't in no show.

                    BOB
          Yes I am, Dad. It's called *Hooray for America!* and I'm
          wearing my costume and I sing and dance and I'm a star.

                    DAD (V.O.)
          You ain't no star of nothing. You ain't wearin' no
          costume and you ain't singin' and you ain't dancin' at
          nobody.

                    BOB
          I'm sorry I ever called you!

                    DAD (V.O.)
          You ain't sorry, and you never called no one.

>   BOB
>   Good-bye. I love...

His Dad hangs up.

>   BOB (CONT'D)
>   ...you.

Bob hangs up.

>   DAVID
>   Hey, toss me that warm-up cream!

Bob tosses David a tube of "James Lipton's Warm-Up Cream." Bob notices someone at the exit door and solemnly nods to David.

>   BOB
>   David—

David turns. In the doorway is the sweetest little KOREAN BOY in a wheelchair. (His feet are particularly fat.) He squeezes the bulb of a squeaky horn mounted on the wheelchair.

(NOTE: CHOW'S voice is obviously, and poorly, overdubbed by David.)

>   CHOW
>   Uncle! Uncle!

>   DAVID
>   Hey, Chow-Chow! How's my favorite nephew?

Chow laughs and holds his hands out.

>   CHOW
>   Slap me ten!

David slaps him ten.

>   CHOW (CONT'D)
>   (suddenly sad)
>   Uncle, I'm sad.

>   DAVID
>   Why's that?

> CHOW
> The doctor says I need special shoes for my fat feet. So
> I can be like a normal kid and run and play.

David squats down next to the kid. Bob watches with pity.

MUSIC: Sad melody

> DAVID
> Hey, no tears. Listen kiddo, I'll tell you what. I'm
> gonna go out there, and I'm gonna be a big star. A
> superstar!

> CHOW
> Yeah?

> DAVID
> Let me finish. And I'm gonna be rich, and have a big
> house with fountains and imported cheeses. I'm gonna
> spend money like M.C. Hammer on crack.

> CHOW
> Will you buy me the special shoes?

> DAVID
> Listen! Zip it! One more interruption and...well,
> you've been warned. I'm gonna have horses, and a car for
> every horse, with a fountain in it.

Bob, wiping tears, grabs David's shoulder.

> BOB
> David...it's showtime.

> DAVID
> (to the kid)
> I'm gonna party so hard and so much, I'm gonna be your
> worst nightmare!

The TEENAGE STAGEHAND leans in.

> TEENAGE STAGEHAND
> Hey guys, guess what! There's word on the street that
> a Hollywood Talent Guy is in the audience tonight.

Supposedly they're looking for a big part. At least,
that's what Mr. Catalanano heard.

Bob and David look at each other with wide eyes.

> BOB
> This is great! I hope you get it!

> DAVID
> I hope I get it, too, Bob!

DIP TO BLACK

AND WE HEAR A FAMILIAR VOICE . . .

> PIT PAT (V.O.)
> Take it from me, I love you!

EXT. FANCY HI-RISE OFFICE BUILDING

SUPER, LOWER THIRD: "**GLOBO-CHEM HEADQUARTERS**" and then "**THREE WEEKS
EARLIER**"

> ANNOUNCER (V.O.)
> Wherever you see Pit Pat, you know you're getting Globo-
> Chem quality, and that you are part of a wonderful,
> worldwide corporation.

MUSIC: Ominous

DISSOLVE TO:

INT. GLOBO-CHEM - CONFERENCE ROOM

A modern, charmless high-tech conference room. We'll return here so
often, let's take a second to describe it. It's got a big conference table
in the center; it's a dark room with only one or two tiny windows that
let out to a roof courtyard. There is a small bank of VIDEO MONITORS and
CLOCKS set to times around the world. MR. HARTNUT is meeting with FOUR
YOUNG EXECUTIVES: CHET, JANE, TODD, and RON.

> MR. HARTNUT
> What do you got for me?

                        JANE
            Well, the elections are fast approaching, sir. Here's a
            recap...

Jane presses a button and the lights go down. A video monitor comes on
with the following commercial...

                                                    FADE TO BLACK.

UP ON: TV COMMERCIAL

A TV commercial using news footage of two candidates for president. The
candidates are DON and DAN, they are nearly identical, forty-five-year-old
white men.

                        ANNOUNCER (V.O.)
            America has an important choice to make in this fall's
            presidential election. A choice that demands facts, not
            propaganda.

As the announcer lists each new "fact," we see the words come up in
GRAPHIC on the bottom third of the screen. There are mild differences
between the two men, but each time a difference comes up, it is
highlighted. (Underlined here.)

                        ANNOUNCER (V.O.)
            Democratic candidate Don McGuthers was an astronaut
            and walked on the moon. Republican Dan McGuffree was
            an astronaut who walked on the moon and rode in a moon
            buggy. Democrat Don has been married for seventeen years
            and has three children. Republican Dan has been married
            for seventeen years and has four children. Democrat Don
            has been a Congressman for thirteen years. Republican
            Dan has been a congressman for fifteen years. America,
            the choice is clear: Republican Dan McGuffree for
            president, because experience really does matter.

SUPER: "EXPERIENCE REALLY DOES MATTER"

WE PULL OUT FROM A TV SCREEN BACK TO THE ROOM...

                        JANE
            While we'd slightly prefer McGuffree, because of his
            horse farm, neither candidate has a definable ethos,

both have enthusiastically cooperated with the corporate
community in the past and would be happy to have our
support.

>   CHET
>   So, who's in the lead?

>   JANE
>   It's fifty-fifty. Anything can happen.

>   TODD
>   Well then we better back both of them, just to be sure.

>   CHET
>   Sure, then we can go halvsies with other companies.

>   RON
>   Halvsies is great. We won't have carte blanche, but . . .

>   CHET
>   Do we even need a president? We've got sixty-two
>   senators and representatives comin' out the ying-yang.

>   HARTNUT
>   It's not good enough. Not for this.

>   JANE
>   If I may ask, sir, for what?

Hartnut hesitates . . . this is a big reveal, then—

>   HARTNUT
>   Operation Green Meadow.

Quiet gasps as we see this gets everyone's rapt attention.

>   JANE
>   (somber)
>   So it's real.

>   HARTNUT
>   Very. My great-grandfather came to America with nothing
>   but a nickel in his pocket, a million dollars in the
>   bank, and a dream: to sell Indians the land they lived

on. Well I'm dreaming, too. I dream of a better world for better people. And I don't want anybody to veto my dream. By God, I'm going to do something I should have done when I was a kid. I'm going to make my own president.

Hartnut speaks into his intercom.

> HARTNUT (CONT'D)
> (to intercom)
> Dini, get me Chance Nightly!

GO TO SPLIT SCREEN

On one side is HARTNUT and the EXECS, the other is Bob as CHANCE NIGHTLY, a James Carville type, but a little flashier. He is sitting on the porch of a shack in the bayou.

SPLIT SCREEN W/EXT. SHACK IN THE BAYOU

> CHANCE
> What all can I do for you?

> HARTNUT
> Make me a president.

> CHANCE
> Well, now I'm 'bout out of that business, you know. Tired of all the kicking and scratchin'.

> HARTNUT
> Hell, you got the last three presidents elected, didn't ya?

> CHANCE
> I might maybe did...

> CHET
> Chance, this would be your best opportunity yet.

No response.

                    JANE
Chance, this is Jane. You pick the man, you mold him,
you make him...

                    TODD
From scratch.

                    HARTNUT
Unlimited funds.

                    CHANCE
Mmmmm...well I tell ya, crawfish season just started,
'n I'm just all pooped up down here. I'm a poopy-butt.

                    HARTNUT
We understand, but if you don't do this, I'll have to
kill you.

                    CHANCE
Hm. I'll need a squirrel patch full of money.

                                                    CUT TO:

INT. AIRPLANE

Chance is on a private jet, having a drink, talking on the phone. He is
all business.

SUPER, LOWER THIRD: **TWO WEEKS AFTER THAT**

                    CHANCE
Listen up, times have changed. It ain't going to be
a politician at all. We gon' find ourselves a clean
slate, a blank tablet, an empty vessel, which we can
fill. What I'm talking about is an actor. And not one'a
the seven or so good ones neither. I'm gon' find me the
most patriotic actor in the United States...no, not
Hollywood! I just said "patriotic"! Trust me, I know
just where to look.

                                                    CUT TO:

EXT. BRANSON, MO., TOWN SIGN

Chance's limo drives by, into town. It passes a large sinkhole with police tape surrounding it. A sign reads: DANGER: SINKHOLE

GRAPHIC: TWO DAYS LATER

MONTAGE - CHANCE going into various shows, we see each marquee as he does so.

MARQUEE - JOSEPH CATALANANO in "ELEANOR ROOSEVELT—BELIEVE IT OR NOT!"

MARQUEE - TRILL HULLSBY in "CHEER FOR AMERICA—A CELEBRATION IN SONG"

MARQUEE - DAVID BUTTERBY in "LINCOLN—MAN OF PASSION AND ROMANCE!"

EXT. "THE BOB AND DAVID BIG FOAM FINGER CELEBRATION THEATRE"

This is the theatre where we were backstage, and we are back in the present tense.

It's a sunny day in Branson, Mo. But the theatre is more run-down than quaint. The big foam fingers with "America's #1" on them are tattered and faded from the weather.

SUPER, LOWER THIRD: ONE WEEK LATER...WHICH IS TO SAY...RIGHT NOW!

Chance Nightly walks into frame, glances up at the big foam finger marquee, laughs to himself—this will be entertaining, at least—and enters.

INT. THE BOB AND DAVID BIG FOAM FINGER CELEBRATION THEATRE

MUSIC: Patriotic backing

Some shots of our AUDIENCE, comprised of pasty overweight VACATIONING FAMILIES in various states of boredom and food digestion, as well as some chattery RETIREES, fill half the seats. Chance takes a seat in the back.

We hear an opening announcement.

                    BOB (LIVE V.O.)
          Ladies and gentlemen, the show you are about to see is
          rated quadruple-X for Xtra Patriotic, Xtra Entertaining,
          Xtra Educational, and adult language and brief nudity.

David runs, jumps on a mini-tramp, flips and lands on the stage.

> DAVID
> Hello, Branson! Let me hear you make some noise!

The small crowd applauds. Bob runs, jumps on the mini-tramp, and lands awkwardly on David's shoulders.

> BOB
> Hooray for America!

They dance as they sing.

> BOB AND DAVID
> (singing to the tune of "Let It Whip")
> The pilgrims landed
> They said all right
> Let's make a country
> If it take us all night
> Let Freedom Rip
> Let Freedom Rip

DISSOLVE TO:

INT. SAME - LATER

David is in a George Washington costume, doing the *Dorf on Golf* gimmick, his tiny legs resting on a table in front of him. Bob, as Abe Lincoln, is standing.

> BOB
> Hey George, how ya doin'?

Bob slaps David on the back and David does a "Dorf-like" fall.

CUTAWAYS TO AUDIENCE. OLD WOMEN AND CHILDREN LAUGHING.

> DAVID
> Heyyy.
> (slow burn)
> Oh hello, Abe Lincoln, the sixteenth president.

> BOB
> Say, I thought you'd be happy to see me.

> DAVID
> Why should I be happy? I was the shortest president, my
> teeth were made of wood, and you tore my country in two!

CUTAWAY TO:

In the audience a small group of HIGH-SCHOOLERS make notes, and behind
them stands an older, strange, long-haired gangly fellow named DINO. He
stares intently, watching Bob and David.

> BOB
> Hey, I got a bad rap for that, but now, I got a good rap
> for that . . .

Onstage, the lights change, David runs off. Bob picks up a cardboard prop
shaped like a mini-Humvee. It says "Hummer" on it.

MUSIC: Gangster rap

> BOB (CONT'D)
> Damn, it's me G. A.B.E. to the L.I.N.C. Doin' a drive-by
> on slizzavery.

Bob pulls out a gun.

> BOB (CONT'D)
> That's right. Got my gat upside the hat of that stupid
> wack-ass beeyatch, inequality.

Bob shoots at the audience.

SFX: Series of startlingly loud gunshots.

Frightened grandmas shriek. The teenagers laugh and shake their heads at
this corny rap.

> BOB (CONT'D)
> Take that, you punk-ass ho'!
>   (to audience)
> It's all good.

SFX: A car peeling out.

BOB with his cardboard car, leaves the stage with swagger.

ANGLE ON: CHANCE NIGHTLY IN THE AUDIENCE, INTRIGUED.

DISSOLVE TO:

INT. SAME - LATER

It's the finale, Bob is onstage, wrapped in an American flag. He sings a lonely, triumphant, "Wind Beneath My Wings" type of song. CUTAWAYS to emotional GRANDMAS and bored TEENS.

>   BOB
> If everyone will be quiet now, I will be so honored as
> to sing the final song of our show. Let's remember the
> troops, wherever they are, whatever country they fight
> for, even our enemies, for without them our troops would
> be unemployed slackers. ALL troops everywhere deserve
> the biggest American thumbs-ups we can give them. Amen.
>   (singing)
> I am the wing of an eagle, of my country I must brag,
> 'cause I was born an American, and I am the wind that
> flaps the flag.

ANGLE ON: Chance making notes, very intrigued by Bob. Could this be America's most patriotic actor?

On the final line, Bob's voice goes impossibly high like a castrato's...

>   BOB (CONT'D)
> I am the wind that flaps the flag.

SFX: Fireworks.

MUSIC: Up-tempo, crazy Keystone Kops melody

Spotlights swing everywhichway. David roller-skates onstage holding sparklers, and sings the crazy final verse.

>   DAVID
>   (singing)
> And that's the story of, and that's the glory of, there
> ain't no more-ey of, we've mined the quarry of...
> America!

              BOB AND DAVID
      And many more!

Bob and David throw cream pies at each other, laughing hysterically, out of character.

Applause. Bob and David bow.

              DAVID
      Good night, Branson. See ya in twenty minutes!

                                          DISSOLVE TO:

EXT. BACKSTAGE - MOMENTS LATER

Bob and David are in street clothes signing autographs. David is signing an autograph for an EXCITED GRANDMA FAN.

              GRANDMA
      Oh, Bob, you were wonderful, and my grandson loved it.

              GRANDSON
      Ha ha. You were funny!

              DAVID
      Thanks, but I'm not Bob.

Bob is speaking to TWO ANNOYED TEENAGERS.

              BOB
      You realize I'm interpreting Lincoln, we don't know how
      he sounded, this was the eighteen-somethings...

              TEEN ONE
      Yeah, hey, David, can you sign my credit slip?

              BOB
      Sure, but I'm not David, but...

              TEEN TWO
      Just initial where it says we stayed for the whole show.

Bob initials the slip. Back to David.

                        GRANDMA
             (getting closer to David)
     So, uh, Bob, I really liked it.

                        DAVID
     Okay, but I'm not . . .

The Grandma's GRANDSON pipes up.

                       GRANDSON
     Can we go now?

                        GRANDMA
     Just a second, Grandma's talking to the performer.
             (to David)
     So, where do you two hang out after the show? I'd love
     to get together . . . party . . . or whatever.

David and Grandma have a moment. Chance Nightly is nearby, watching.

                        DAVID
     I just don't know . . .

                        GRANDMA
     Bob, come on.

                        DAVID
     Okay, okay, just come looking for me, then. I'm *Bob
     Odenkirk* . . .

Chance makes notes as David speaks.

                   DAVID (CONT'D)
     —And I'll be at the Stage Canteen tonight after the
     tenth show.

Grandma nods, sexily. Chance has the notes he needs and turns to go.

ANGLE ON: TEENAGE STAGEHAND leaning out the backstage door.

                TEENAGE STAGEHAND
     Bob, David, next show is in fifteen minutes!

WIDE SHOT: The audience dispersing, Bob and David heading back in for
their umpteenth show of the day, Chance walking past camera, his mind
spinning.

INT. BACKSTAGE

Bob and David come in, Bob is burning with energy.

> BOB
> David, man, we're a hit! We gotta do what I said.

> DAVID
> A reunion tour?

> BOB
> No, you're getting way ahead of yourself. We gotta go
> into Mr. Billups's office and get paid. Remember, we want
> gross points on profit, not a *percentage!*

Bob takes David down a thin, dark passage to stand outside a cruddy door
marked "Theatre Office."

> DAVID
> Okay yeah. Oh, and I need to use the real U.S.
> Constitution for my magic trick, I think people can tell
> I'm using a fake one.

> BOB
> Right, and bigger dressing room.

> DAVID
> Oh, and clothing pegs to hang clothes on!

> BOB
> And red M&M's. Only red. Remember where we're headed?

> DAVID
> The tip of . . . something.

> BOB
> Top.

> DAVID
> The tip of the top.

                    BOB
Of the . . . mmmmm.

                    DAVID
Mip! The tip of the mip!

                    BOB
The tip-top of the mip-mop!

                    DAVID
Mop!

                    BOB
What about a mop?

                    DAVID
Nothing. You go first.

They open the creaky door and enter—

INT. THEATER OFFICE

A shitty, overstuffed hoarders theatre office. The OWNER sits behind an
old-style calculating machine, counting dirty dollar bills and doing
sums.

                    BOB
Uh . . . Mr. Billups?

                    DAVID
Mr. B . . . Sir?

Bob clears his throat. No response. David claps his hand and YIPS.

                    DAVID (CONT'D)
Yip!!

The OWNER turns, mechanically, to face them. We see that it is a
MECHANICAL BEAR. But Bob and David don't notice this.

                    BEAR
Oh, ho ho ho, hee hee hee, it's a bear's banjo life
for me!

                        DAVID
            That's great, Mr. Billups.

David looks at Bob—what's up?

                        BOB
            Mr. Billups...uh, we wanted to talk to you about a
            raise. We want a raise. We DEMAND a raise.

                        DAVID
            Yes, we want gross points.

                        BOB
            Also, I think you've turned into a mechanical bear.

The mechanical bear smiles at them and says:

                        BEAR
            That's all, folks!

And chuckles. Bob and David share a curious look, then DINO, the hippy
who was standing near the teenagers earlier, steps from behind the
mechanical bear. He is operating the bear with a control panel. Bob and
David turn to see the crotchety MR. BILLUPS, the owner, standing off to
the side, clapping.

                        DAVID
            Oh, hello, Mr. Billups.

                        MR. BILLUPS
            Boys, please, don't sit down. I have some terrific news,
            for me. I'm going to let you boys go.

                        DAVID
            Where?

                        MR. BILLUPS
            Anywhere you want.

Bob and David are momentarily thrilled.

                        MR. BILLUPS (CONT'D)
            You're fired.
                    (turning to Dino)

I will take the family of mechanical bear puppets.

> DINO
> They're not PUPPETS! They're anima-motron-simulacs!

> MR. BILLUPS
> Uh-huh. Have 'em ready to go in ten. Minutes.

Bob and David cast a withering look at the gleeful Dino.

EXT. BRANSON

Bob and David walk through the streets of Branson, passing numerous sinkholes that are surrounded by police tape and blinking metal barriers.

> BOB
> Man, how am I going to tell my parents I was fired from a show they didn't believe I was in!

David is getting emotional, we can tell by his snuffling.

> BOB (CONT'D)
> Uh oh...

David's tearful snuffling builds.

> BOB (CONT'D)
> Don't cry, David. Don't...it's embarrassing...

David can't help himself. He starts bawling and he sounds JUST LIKE A BABY! Overdubbed with a real baby's cry.

> BOB (CONT'D)
> Sh...David...come here...come on...

Bob takes David aside, away from any onlookers to help him get it together.

> BOB (CONT'D)
> David, stop. Come on...is this about getting fired?

David nods.

>   BOB (CONT'D)
>   David, we're not done, okay? I mean, remember the
>   coattail theory?

David does not.

>   BOB (CONT'D)
>   Well, it's this, when a performer goes into show
>   business they are wearing a very small coat. It has no
>   tails. It's like a light windbreaker. But as they get
>   more famous that coat grows warmer and begins to grow
>   tails, like a sea-fish. Well, we're a team, and that
>   means we have three coats—yours, mine, and the team
>   coat. If you get more famous than I do, then I pull on
>   your tails to yank myself up, if I get more famous than
>   you, then you clamber up my tail, and if we both get
>   famous we chop that tail off and fuck everyone else.
>   Okay?

David nods, feeling all better. They begin walking.

>   BOB (CONT'D)
>   Great. Look around you. What do you see?

We see what David sees: a bleak country town, mostly boarded up, with a
lot of sinkholes. Although they look as if maybe they were dug into the
earth.

>   DAVID
>   A bunch of holes full of nothing!

>   BOB
>   Those aren't holes, David! They're opportunities for
>   success! Who knows? You could fall into one of those
>   holes and come out on top of the world!

>   DAVID
>   In China?

>   BOB
>   No, in America. Success can come from anywhere at any
>   time.

                    DAVID
     I guess...as long as there's a TV camera nearby.

                    BOB
     That's the spirit. Come on, I'll buy you a beer slushy.

David smiles and the two walk on down the street bustling with performers
and tourists.

                                                                  CUT TO:

INT. GLOBO-CHEM MEETING ROOM

RON and JANE are looking out the window.

                    JANE
     What could Mr. Hartnut be planning?

                    RON
     The man's a genius. He does his best thinking in that
     suit.

They are looking down at the Atrium outdoor area where someone is walking
around in a big powder-blue suit, like a team mascot wears.

EXT. ATRIUM - CONTINUOUS

Mr. Hartnut in the PIT PAT MASCOT COSTUME is pacing, brooding, and
occasionally scratching his furry big head. We continue to hear Ron and
Jane's conversation.

                    RON (V.O.)
     He says he can get away from everything in there. No
     noise, no distractions.

                    JANE (V.O.)
     And people like him when he's wearing it. Strangers wave
     to him.

A STRANGER in the quad area, eating lunch, looks up at the big blue
mascot and waves awkwardly. Pit Pat waves back.

                    RON (V.O.)
     God, it must stink in there.

EXT. BAR

A local bar in Branson. The sign says, "Rick's Bar—Bringing Actors and Drinks Together for over Ten Years."

INT. RICK'S BAR

There are a BUNCH OF ACTOR TYPES drinking. Some of them wear funny patriotic outfits, some look like famous historical figures.

JOSEPH CATALANANO is a mustached, pompous actor in Eleanor Roosevelt drag.

TRILL is an impossibly upbeat, swishy fellow of indeterminate age, with freckles and a quiff, wearing a varsity jersey. DRAKE is a fat, slovenly fellow who looks sort of like an Osmond brother.

OVERTON, the friendly bartender, takes note as Bob and David enter.

                  OVERTON
        Hey everybody, it's Bob and David.

Everybody in the bar responds with hearty hellos—

               BOB AND DAVID
       Hey. Hey Stu, Pete, Jenny. Hi, Trill.

                  OVERTON
       What's up, guys? It's only six o'clock. Don't you have
       seven more shows tonight?

                  BOB
   No.

                  DAVID
       Yeah, we quit.

People nod . . . they're used to this.

                  BOB
       What about you, Trill?

                    TRILL
              (pompous)
     Oh, I quit my show, too. From now on I'm just going to
     direct major feature films.

                    BOB
     Sure, why not? Mr. Catalanano, did you quit, too?

Mr. Catalanano sadly nods.

                    BOB (CONT'D)
     What about your one man show about "Eleanor Roosevelt"?

                    JOSEPH
              (actorly, overly grand)
     Yes, the role was beginning to overtake me, so I, too,
     as well, and also, vacated my employ.

Bob and David doubt his story.

                    BOB
     Drake, aren't you performing *One Bad Apple* your solo
     tribute to the Osmond family tonight?

                    DRAKE
     No, I was replaced.

                    DAVID
     That's impossible! Who looks more like an Osmond than
     you?!

We see DRAKE up close, he looks like an Osmond who melted.

                    DRAKE
     Apparently a mechanical bear does.

Bob and David shake their heads.

                    DRAKE (CONT'D)
     They said no one would know the difference.

                    BOB
     We were replaced by mechanical bears, too.

>   TRILL
> Me three.

>   JOSEPH
> Myself, as well, also, too.

Overton leans over the bar, speaking assuredly. People share skeptical looks during his speech.

>   OVERTON
> It's all a part of the plan, gentlemen. "Operation Dwindlestick." First you replace the actors with mechanical bears, then you replace the audience with mechanical bears, then you replace the mechanical bears with mechanical apes because what the hell do mechanical bears know!

>   BOB
> So then you just have a bunch of mechanical bears performing for mechanical apes?

>   OVERTON
>   (scoffs)
> Do the math. Eat the worm.

This is making a lot of sense to the assembled dopes.

>   DAVID
> What's the endgame? Who does it benefit?

>   OVERTON
> It's all a sideshow, don't you see? A distraction from the real swindle. What do you think those holes outside are about? You see any dirt piles by those holes? The president's going to live underground within two years. They got a water-powered car and plans to build a golf course on the moon.

The assembled audience of dim-bulbs is still with him, but he takes it a step too far—

>   OVERTON (CONT'D)
> Oh, and the biggest scam of them all?...Porn stars use fake names.

The mob reacts with shock and skepticism, shaking heads, rolling eyes. Bob expresses their shared thought—

>   BOB
>   You're nuts.

>   OVERTON
>   Yeah, I'm nuts. Big Brother is laughin', boys and girls,
>   and you're getting your news from Jay Leno.

>   BOB
>   Well, Jay's funny.

>   DAVID
>   Yeah...so...we're laughing, too.

>   BOB
>   So everyone's laughing. That's good, right?

Overton shakes his head and walks away.

>   JOSEPH
>   Say, has anyone heard if that talent agent stopped by? I
>   think he was in my show...I heard someone coughing.

>   DRAKE
>   That was me. My doctor said I'm allergic to dust...and
>   female impersonators.

MUSIC: Foreboding score plays under next two scenes

                                                        DISS. TO:

INT. CONFERENCE ROOM

Hartnut (still in the Pit-Pat costume) stands at the head of the conference table, JANE and RON and OTHER EXECS are gathered around, quietly awaiting some order.

Hartnut dramatically removes the Pit-Pat mascot head, revealing his own face. He has been sweating and his hair is matted and greasy. A housefly buzzes out from under the mascot head. Ron and Jane share a queasy look.

                    RON
          What is it, Mr. Hartnut?

                    HARTNUT
          Rocket fuel.

                    JANE
          What about rocket fuel, sir?

                    HARTNUT
          We need some.

                    RON
          How much?

                    HARTNUT
          TWENTY-EIGHT STORIES' WORTH.

Ron and Jane look to each other, confused, OFF THIS WE

                                                    DISS. TO:

INT. BRANSON CHAIN HOTEL - "THE YE'OLD BESTE TOWNE INNE HOTEL"

LINDA, CHANCE'S ASSISTANT is checking them in. CHANCE looks on with
contempt at a FAT TOURIST KID standing nearby sloppily eating a churro.

                                                    DISS. TO:

EXT. BAR

Everyone is saying good-bye, dispersing. Bob and David are last.

                    BOB
          Bye, Mr. Catalanano. Bye, Trill.

                    TRILL
          Bye, Bob and David. Remember, tomorrow's another day...

                    DAVID
          Thanks, T.

Bob and David hesitate, this is a make-or-break moment.

                    BOB
Well, this is it, I guess.

                    DAVID
The tip-top of the mip-mop?

                    BOB
No, the end. Of us.

                    DAVID
Why?

                    BOB
Well, we got fired. I mean, I figure you want to go
pursue your dreams of becoming a junkie and having a
reality show about you.

                    DAVID
Yeah, I guess. And you'll probably join that cult and
have that reality show about you.

                    BOB
Yeah. Hey...

David stops, Bob stares at him.

                    DAVID
What?

Emotionally—

                    BOB
Good luck with your reality show.

                    DAVID
Thanks. And Bob...

                    BOB
What?
     (beat)
What do you want to tell me? You can say it, you can say
anything...

                    DAVID
          It's just, well...Good luck.

                    BOB
          With what?

                    DAVID
          Your reality show.

                    BOB
          Oh, thanks. Thanks, David. That means a lot coming from
          you.

They resume their walk and David immediately falls into a hole, but Bob
doesn't see this...he just keeps walking and talking...

                    BOB (CONT'D)
          Seeing as how you'll have a reality show, too, and we
          might be up against each other someday, same time slot
          and all...that's really big of you, David.
                    (beat)
          David?

Bob looks around, no David...

                    BOB (CONT'D)
          David?

Suddenly Bob hears David's baby cry. He walks back, until he finds the
hole David fell in and hears the baby cry coming out of it.

                    BOB (CONT'D)
          David?

                    DAVID (V.O.)
          Down here!

                    BOB
          I...hey...I'll get help.

                    DAVID
          'K. I'll just sit here, quietly.

Bob runs for help, but suddenly stops. His mind is suddenly reeling...on fire with an idea!

>   BOB
>   Uh...wait, no...don't do that. Cry, David. Cry like a
>   baby. Cry like the biggest baby you ever were in your
>   life! I got an idea!

David starts baby-bawling.

>   BOB (CONT'D)
>   (to himself)
>   This is gonna make that Lindbergh baby look like an idiot!

>   CUT TO:

A LOCAL NEWS SHOW OPENING MONTAGE - THAT NIGHT

THIS MONTAGE CONSISTS OF: A FARMER BEING INTERVIEWED AGAINST A FIELD, THEN A SHOT OF THE FIELD, AND REPEAT THESE TWO SHOTS.

MUSIC: Local TV news theme

>   ANNOUNCER (V.O.)
>   You're watching Channel Three local news. Here's Carl
>   Trundle with the day's events...

CARL is a typical middle-aged local news guy. Straight delivery...

>   CARL
>   Good evening. Our top stories: Fudge Season officially
>   begins tomorrow night at sundown. We'll have a full
>   report later, but first, the story that has captivated
>   our town today; the little baby girl trapped in a hole
>   and the courageous young man who reported it to an
>   emergency operator this evening. On the scene is our
>   own Lisa Dunnandan. Lisa?

>   CUT TO:

EXT. HOLE - NIGHT

The area is lit with emergency lighting. PEOPLE and EMERGENCY WORKERS are gathered.

                    LISA
        Carl, rescue crews are trying desperately to free the
        little girl who you can hear crying down in the hole.
        Listen...

She holds the microphone out, we hear what sounds like a very young child
or even a baby, crying.

                    LISA (CONT'D)
        It's a parent's worst nightmare. Thank God for the
        young man whose quick thinking may save her, Mr. Bob
        Ofenklerp.

Bob is wrapped in a blanket, shivering, and sipping hot cocoa. The small
crowd listens respectfully when he talks.

                    BOB
        Hi, good to be here. How's everybody doin'?

                    LISA
        Bob, what did you think when you heard the sound of this
        baby crying?

                    BOB
        I knew that this was a true tragedy that should be
        televised. This is very hard for me. Please ask me
        another question.

                    LISA
        Now we have a recording of the phone call you made only
        minutes ago. Let's listen to that now...

SUPER LOWER THIRD: SUBTITLES OF THE PHONE CALL AND A PICTURE OF A
TELEPHONE.

SUPER: "HERO'S PHONE CALL"

                    OPERATOR (V.O.)
        9-1-1, my name is Shawntel, I'll be your emergency
        representative. Anything you need today, just ask for
        Shawntel.

                    BOB (V.O.)
        Oh my God, terrible trouble.

                    OPERATOR (V.O.)
Well, you called the right place, sir. We've been helping
people for over thirty years. R U in trouble? 9-1-1 is on
the double.

                    BOB (V.O.)
Listen, sir.

                    OPERATOR (V.O.)
Please, call me Shawntel.

                    BOB (V.O.)
Uh, all right Shawntel. It sounds like a baby is trapped
in a hole. You've got to get a TV crew here as soon as
possible. Oh my God.

                    OPERATOR (V.O.)
Well, I will see what I can do for you. Are you in the
market for some speakers?

Lose subtitles and photos, full on Lisa and Bob at the scene.

                    LISA
Bob, some people are calling you a hero for what you've
done. What do you say?

                    BOB
I'd like to say that I'm no hero, I'm just an
American...

                                                    CUT TO:

CLOSE-UP ON A TV IN A HOTEL ROOM

As Bob makes his patriotic speech on the TV, we slowly reveal that Chance
and LINDA, his assistant, are in this hotel room, fucking.

                    BOB (ON TV) (CONT'D)
        (referring to the crowd assembled around him)
    Just like you, and you, and all of you watching on TV.

Linda notices Bob on TV, she stops riding chance.

                 LINDA
Wait, Chance, you should see this . . .

Chance looks at the TV. They both grow intrigued by Bob's speech.

                 BOB
Frankly, I'm just a regular fellow. I can't stop caring,
and I can't stop trying, and I can't stop leading. It's
simple; I can't stop being an American. Hooray for
America!

The crowd around Bob cheers, pats him on the back.

                 CROWD
Hurray!

Chance grins and pushes Linda aside. Chance runs over to the window. This
is literally happening just below his room.

                 CHANCE
I think I found my pickle-lilly. Sugar bush, get Hartnut
on the phone. Tell him I done did done it.

                                       CUT TO:

EXT. RESCUE SITE - CONTINUOUS

Behind Bob and the Reporter there is a hubbub from the emergency crew.

                 WORKERS (O.S.)
We got her!

The CROWD falls silent, anxiously awaiting the appearance of the baby
girl. Workers crank a crane. The crying grows louder.

                 LISA
             (sotto)
We're about to get our first glimpse of the precious
baby girl who has been trapped for God knows how
long . . .

It's not a baby. It's David, covered in muddy muck, wearing shorts that
look a bit like diapers *(Needs to be in shorts in earlier scenes). He is
lifted into view.

EXT. HOLE

When David realizes he's out of the hole, his crying turns into soft coos.

>   DAVID
>   Ahhh, ahhh, mmmm, oooh. Hmmm.
>
>   (noticing crowd)
>   Hello.

David and Bob share a look. David glances around at all the cameras and the crowd.

>   DAVID (CONT'D)
>   Hey, it worked!

A rescue WORKER pipes up.

>   WORKER
>   What the hell?

THE REPORTER gets serious with Bob.

>   LISA
>   Mr. Olenklep, did you know that that wasn't a baby in
>   that hole?

Bob doesn't know what to say . . . he got his moment, but he doesn't quite know what to do with it, so . . . he runs away. People are confused and angry. They turn to David, who can't move because he's rigged to the rescue crane.

>   LISA (CONT'D)
>   It looks like we've all been victims of a very cruel
>   prank.

Workers and onlookers gather around David, menacingly. Lisa pokes her microphone into David's face.

>   LISA (CONT'D)
>   You! What's your name?

>   DAVID
>   Uh . . . David Cross. Hello.

                 LISA
What were you doing in that hole? Pranking everyone?

                 DAVID
No...uh, no. Not at all. This is the first I'm hearing
about all of this, myself. I mean, I was in the hole,
so...I was out of the loop. No information could get to
me. Frankly, I am as upset as anyone.

No one is quite sure how to take this, but suddenly we hear someone
applauding and the camera swings over to find Chance, running up as he
buckles his pants. He runs right up next to David.

                 CHANCE
Well said, let's hear it for him, folks! This kid braved
the odds. He's an American hero!

The mob is unsure of this pitch, but there is some applause.

                 LISA
Who are you, sir?

                 CHANCE
I'm just a person—just a person who can spot a hero when
he rises up out of the dirt to bring us all together
and remind us of who we are—the best country God ever
wished into being. Let's hear it for the hero!

General applause grows to rousing applause.

                 DAVID
              (meekly)
That's me.

Amidst the hubbub, Chance is smiling and laughing. David begins to smile
and laugh, too...and Chance turns to David and says:

                 CHANCE
Young man, you the coffee bean atop my tomato pancake!

The rousing applause of the crowd for David carries over as we...

                                     DISSOLVE TO:

EXT. BAR - THE NEXT DAY

Rousing applause from inside—

INT. BAR

All the actors we met a day ago are cheering, David is in the middle of the group—

A banner reads, "Congratulations and Good Luck, David." TRILL toasts him.

                    TRILL
               (overly excited)
          To David, the man who got the part!

Assembled actors all raise their glasses and cheer through gritted teeth, barely concealing their jealousy. David doesn't notice.

                    TRILL (CONT'D)
          ...that he didn't even have to audition for!
               (weak laughter)
Joseph Catalanano steps up—

                    JOSEPH
          May I say a few words, David?

                    DAVID
          Mr. Catalanano, I'd be honored.

Joseph puts reading glasses on, although he doesn't read anything.

                    JOSEPH
          David, as Joseph Catalanano once said, no one is happier
          for an actor who gets a role than his fellow actors.

Murmurs of agreement. Joseph removes his reading glasses.

                    DAVID
          Thanks.

                    TRILL
          David, seriously, when I first saw you, I thought, this
          kid, this one, he needs work. Really. And you must've
          gone and did it, 'cause dammit, kid...

> (losing the thread)
> ...make us proud!

Weaker cheers. Trill gives David a slightly painful, angry kiss.

> DAVID
>
> Wow!

A PATRIOTIC SHOWGIRL steps up.

> PATRIOTIC SHOWGIRL
>
> We got you this.

She hands him a book wrapped in drama mask paper. He opens it and reads the title...

> DAVID
>
> *Five minutes, Mr. Catalanano: The Joseph Catalanano Story.*

> PATRIOTIC SHOWGIRL
>
> Joseph picked it out.

> JOSEPH
>
> It's the only copy there is.

> DAVID
> (sincerely)
> Well, that's great...I'll try not to throw it out.

> JOSEPH
>
> It can't but help.

> TRILL
> If they need an understudy, you know where I am!
> (very emotional)
> Let's cheer again, for David, the man who got the part!
> (a beat, he cries)
> God!

People comfort Trill. Chance leans in from outside.

> CHANCE
>
> Come on, boy!

People follow David out the door, patting him on the back the whole way. Bob is lost in the crowd and shouts out—

> BOB
> David! Don't forget about the coattails!

> DAVID
> (yelling back)
> Oh, no thanks, I'm stuffed!

EXT. BAR

David and Chance get into a long black limousine. The limo has a "Just Nominated" sign on the back and trails cans and ribbons. Everyone waves good-bye. Overton pats Bob on the back.

MUSIC: Upbeat, MOVING ON music takes us into—

INT. PRESS CONFERENCE

CHANCE and a COTERIE of HANDLERS are assembled around a podium in this typical press conference setup.

> CHANCE
> Reporters, press people, thank you for coming. Let's face it, democracy in America has become a joke! It's been reduced to the choice between two barely distinguishable corporate lackeys. Well, no more! Tonight we announce the formation of a truly viable third political party: TCBP—THE COUNTRY'S BEST PARTY!

A PIT PAT MASCOT dances out, holding a banner with TCBP on it.

> CHANCE (CONT'D)
> Now I'd like to introduce our candidate, an unknown, untainted by Washington and its mendicants; Mr. Li'l Davey Cross!

David, grinning, steps up to the microphone as flashbulbs go off. He's ecstatic.

> DAVID
> Hi! First of all, I'm psyched. Secondly, it's time to take this country back from the fat cats on Capitol Hill.

ANGLE: We see David is reading from a teleprompter.

> DAVID (CONT'D)
> Now, I am not from Washington and, if elected, I
> will not go there. Thank you. This is gonna be fun.
> Questions?

> REPORTER ONE
> David, you've never held office, what qualifies you for
> the presidency?

> DAVID
> I am not a politician!

CUT TO:

TV INFOMERCIAL OPENING TITLE SEQUENCE

SFX: Loud, synth infomercial music up.

Over the Title Graphic "Amazing People," video clips of David in various
situations fly across the screen: kissing a baby, pinning a medal on an
old soldier, saluting a flag and crying, on a parasail, smiling to camera,
and lastly, using a mop.

> ANNOUNCER (V.O.)
> Tonight, on *Amazing People*, we'll meet a candidate for
> president of the United States who will save you time
> and money, and make your life a lot easier. Now here are
> your hosts, Nancy Gumphrey and Ernie!

TV INFOMERCIAL SET

A typical cheesy infomercial set. The hosts, NANCY and ERNIE, a fey
Englishman, bound out from backstage to wild applause of a hyperactive,
paid AUDIENCE.

> NANCY
> Hi. How are you, Ernie?

> ERNIE
> I'm pip of the pop, Miss Nancy!

                         NANCY
Well, I can't wait to hear about this new person you've
got for us!

                         ERNIE
Yes. Nancy, what if I told you that I met a candidate for
president who wasn't a Washington insider fat cat?

                         NANCY
That sounds great.

                         ERNIE
And what if I told you that he'll lower taxes, make this
great country great again, and won't put up with any
Washington shenanigans?

                         NANCY
Wow! Well, that sounds great, doesn't it, folks?

CUTAWAY TO AUDIENCE CLAPPING

CUTAWAY TO GLOBO-CHEM MEETING ROOM, Chance, Jane, Ron, and other Execs
are gathered around, watching this tape...

ON VIDEO:

                         ERNIE
But that's not all, step over here.

Ernie drags Nancy over to a table piled high with rancid sponges and mops.

                         ERNIE (CONT'D)
Look at this awful mess.

                         NANCY
      Ewww!

                         ERNIE
These are months-old mildewed sponges, mops, cleaning
rags—but guess what Nancy, what if I told you you could
throw them all away?!

In a grand gesture, Ernie sweeps them all off the table into a garbage
can. TV Audience goes nuts.

                    NANCY
          Wow! I can't wait to meet this guy.

                    ERNIE
          Well, here he comes, folks. David!

David enters to great applause.

                    ERNIE (CONT'D)
          Now when we return we'll watch David take on a real fat
          cat politician.

ANGLE ON: FAT CAT POLITICIAN. A cartoonish guy standing behind a podium.

                    AUDIENCE
          Woooooo!

                    NANCY
          Stay with us!

                                                              CUT TO:

INT. GLOBO-CHEM MEETING ROOM

                    HARTNUT
          You think people will go for it?

                    CHANCE
          People are ready for this. Everybody knows they gettin'
          the show, why not cut loose, let 'em really see one. Call
          a crawfish a crawfish and I think we'll make a sale.

A BEAT.

                    HARTNUT
          Do you think it'll work?

                    CHANCE
          It might-could.

                    HARTNUT
          Hmmm. Do you like that sundae, future president?

Reveal David sitting at the end of the table eating a giant chocolate sundae, his face messy with hot fudge.

> DAVID
> (speaking through a mouthful of ice cream)
> Very much so, thank you, sir.

Smiles all around.

MUSIC PLAYS UNDER THESE SCENES FROM THE CAMPAIGN

CUT TO:

EXT. STREET - DAY

PEOPLE on the street, standing near a poster for David. Talking to camera.

> WOMAN
> I think it's all just a big sales job. It's sick, but, I guess they're all that way.

CUT TO:

> MAN 1
> He hasn't got a snowball's chance. Third parties never win. Underdogs, though, I can relate to. Give him a chance.

CUT TO:

> MAN 2
> I like him. He's like me. He's just a guy. I don't know. He makes me laugh.

INT. RADIO TALK SHOW

Bob as a crazy radio talk show host. A large poster hangs behind him reading: "Tom Rite, WTLK."

> TOM
> (irate)
> Who's buying this?! Who's buying this "David" guy? This guy is a product, he's manufactured. Democracy reduced to merchandising, people. You know it, I know it. It's

been going on for years and this David comes along and
now it's out in the open and I say it's about time! Go
for it. You may be liberal, you may be conservative, but
I'm Rite!

All the phone lines light up.

In one swift movement he signals the engineer; the show music plays, he
drops his headphones, sips his coffee and looks at the paper, totally
disinterested in what he just said.

                                                                CUT TO:

INT. SMALL MEETING HALL

David at the podium. He is taking questions from REGULAR CITIZENS in the
audience. A Pit Pat is nearby, waving.

                    DAVID
          This is a hoot. You, sir!

A COLLEGE PROFESSOR steps up to the audience mic.

                    PROFESSOR
          Yes. I'm Tim Belger, a professor of history at Manute
          College here in town...

                    DAVID
          Okay, I've got to say something. I can't answer your
          question.

                    PROFESSOR
          But I haven't asked it yet.

                    DAVID
          Yes, but I'm not that smart. I never went to college.
          I'm not an intellectual. I'm just a person, an American
          person. You should save your questions for a politician.
          But I'm not one.

Cheers from the crowd.

                    CROWD
          Yeah! You the man!

The crowd taunts the retreating PROFESSOR.

> CROWD (CONT'D)
> You! You! You! You!

CUTAWAY TO A SMILING CHANCE WATCHING FROM OFFSTAGE

> DAVID
> Give him a goodie bag.

A Pit Pat tries to give the sulking Professor a goodie bag; he doesn't take it. A GOOD-LOOKING WOMAN in a sequined sweater steps up to the mic.

> WOMAN
> Uh, yeah, I just think you're adorable. And I saw you on *Good Time Today with Mark and Maura*, and the other guest was Clint Black. Was he nice?

> DAVID
> Thank you. Good question. He's fantastic.

Applause and cheers.

> DAVID (CONT'D)
> Give her a hat and a goodie bag.

Pit Pat hands the Woman a hat and a goodie bag.

CUT TO:

EXT. CAMPAIGN BUS

A red, white, and blue campaign bus with the logo "T.C.B.P." on the side. It's driving down a country road in the Midwest, and David is leaning out the window, waving wildly, to no one.

CUT TO:

EXT. STADIUM

Using found footage of a football game. It's halftime, and a show is taking place on the field.

CLOSE-UP OF ACTION ON THE FIELD

David pops out of a big cake, waves to the crowd and dances with HOT GIRLS and Pit Pats to a marching band.

                                                        CUT TO:

SITCOM SET

In a living room of a typical, live action sitcom show, we see the DAD and MOM adoring their DAUGHTER in her prom dress.

                    DAD
          You are prettier than a princess.

                    MOM
          The last time your dad said that to me we were playing
          Pong.

Canned laughs.

SFX: Knock on door.

                    DAUGHTER
          That's my date, I'm so nervous.

                    MOM
          Well, you were the one who thought a blind date on prom
          night would make "everything more exciting."

Another knock. Dad crosses to the door.

                    DAD
          Here goes nothing.

He opens the door. It's David in a red, white, and blue tuxedo, with roses.

Wild cheers from the studio audience. He thumbs up the audience, then carries on with the scene.

                                                        CUT TO:

INT. GLOBO-CHEM MEETING ROOM

CHANCE, HARTNUT, and the Others are watching the news and the numbers say...

Republican—40%
Democrat—34%
The Country's Best Party—22%

They are happy.

ANGLE ON: David sleeping on the couch, holding a blanket . . . their golden child. Hartnut tousles his hair.

>   CHANCE
> Okay, now tonight's debate is it. I mean it. The whole
> campaign rides on this one.

>   CHET
> Do you think he can pull it off?

>   CHANCE
> Do crayfish shit in the bayou?

Long pause.

>   RON
>   . . . Yes?

INT. AUDITORIUM

The candidates, David, Don, and Dan, are at their podiums. They are all getting final touch-ups for a televised debate. Chance talks to David.

>   CHANCE
> Now you remember what we practiced, right?

>   DAVID
> Yeah. Don't wink and don't make clicking noises. Don't
> sweat, and don't sniff your fingers.

>   CHANCE
> Great. Now remember, you're an *outsider*, you're new to
> this, you don't know everything, but you do know one
> thing.

>   DAVID
> Uh-huh, what is that?

> CHANCE
> I'll tell you later.

A STAGE MANAGER steps out with the countdown, Chance moves off-camera.

CUT TO:

THE DEBATE

The moderator is COBB WOODLAND, a typical network anchorman.

> COBB
> Hello Cobb Woodland here, about to begin the Great
> Debate. Republican Dan McGuffree, your opening
> statement?

DAN MCGUFFREE, the Republican candidate, speaks first.

> DAN
> As an astronaut, I had the distinct pleasure of walking
> on the surface of the moon. This experience taught me
> the values of courage, prudency, and weightlessness.
> Qualities I plan to bring to being your next president.
> Thank you.

SFX: Applause.

> COBB
> Demcoratic nominee, Don McGuthers?

> DON
> Well, Dan, let me say that I, too, was an astronaut, and
> I, too, have been on the moon. I have stood, and sat,
> and even shat, on the moon—
>   (pointedly, to Dan)
> —and you, sir, are no moon man!

SFX: Applause.

> COBB
> And the Country's Best Party candidate, David.

                     DAVID

America. I'm just like all of you. So, won't you vote for
me, and elect yourself "el presidente"? Please say yes.
Love, David.

SFX: Applause.

BEGIN DEBATE MONTAGE

                     DON

...take a three percent cut across the board and
redistribute it to the states.

Applause.

                                    DISSOLVE TO:

                     DAN

...in doing so we'd increase the Pentagon's budget, cut
taxes, and build five hundred new prisons.

Applause.

                                    DISSOLVE TO:

                     DAVID

...after you pay your taxes?! Right?
...how about a "Thank You" from the IRS, or what I like
to call, "The Internal 'Revenue' Service"...
      (rolls his eyes)

Applause.

                  DAVID (CONT'D)

Then we combine prisons and schools, call them
schrizons and you've got some clear motivation for those
kids. Thank you.

Applause mixed with happy hooting.

                                    DISSOLVE TO:

                              DON
                    ...send the ambassador to Cuba, and firmly remind them
                    that democracy is America's number one export.

Applause.

                                                            DISSOLVE TO:

                              DAN
                      (emotional story)
                    ...and that woman's name is Donita Mqueef. She's with
                    us tonight. Stand up, dear.

An elderly black woman in the audience stands, to applause.

                              DAN (CONT'D)
                    We're going to get you that turkey dinner, dear!

                                                            DISSOLVE TO:

                              DAVID
                    ...and so I want you all to join me in checking under
                    your seat. Check under your seat. Who's got the star?

Everyone in the audience checks under their seats. We hear, off-camera...

                              AUDIENCE MEMBER
                    Hey!

Camera swooshes to catch the BLACK FEMALE AUDIENCE MEMBER waving a big
gold star, super-excited!

                                                    ENERGETIC SMASH CUT:

The WOMAN is onstage with David. David is slapping hundred-dollar bills
into her open palm. The AUDIENCE counts along with him.

                              DAVID
                    Three hundred, four hundred, five hundred...

ANGLE ON: Dan and Don are annoyed.

                                                            DISSOLVE TO:

                        DAN
        ...because I believe we can all go forward together,
        only if our leaders are behind us all the way. Now I
        would like to ask a question to David.

David is shocked out of a daydream.

                        DAVID
        Huh? What's up?

                        DAN
        David, the American people deserve to know the
        character of the people they're voting for.

Dan pulls out a blown-up PHOTO.

                        DAN (CONT'D)
        This picture clearly shows you smoking marijuana. What
        do you say?

The audience gasps. In the photo, David is in a DORM ROOM with two other
kids, giving a thumbs-up, his mouth on the BONG. Everyone is very high.

                        DAVID
                    (nervous)
        Okay. Wow. Where'd you get that? Did T.J. give that to
        you? Where is he?

                        DON
        Answer the question.

Chance and Hartnut are nervous.

                        DAVID
        Look, everybody, listen. I'm not going to lie to you.
        Yes, I was in a place where there was marijuana. But,
        the question is, did I in fact inhale?

ANGLE ON: Chance and Hartnut relieved.

                        DAVID (CONT'D)
        Yes. Of course I did.

ANGLE ON: Chance and Hartnut nervous again.

                    DAVID (CONT'D)
          But, let me make one thing perfectly clear. I . . . did
          not . . . get high.

Audience murmurs, they're not really buying it.

                    DAVID (CONT'D)
          It was all shake. By the time the bowl got to me it was
          cashed. It was a beat party, the people I was supposed to
          meet never showed, so I blew it off, got hammered instead.

Murmurs of disapproval. Dan and Don smile. Cobb pounds his gavel.

                    COBB
          The Great Debate will be back after this.

                    STAGEHAND (O.S.)
          Clear!

Chance approaches David.

                    DAVID
          How am I doing? These guys are killing with their moon
          material.

                    CHANCE
          Don't worry about them, they can go on about the moon
          all they want. You just read this.

Chance hands David a script. David's eyes widen as he reads.

MOMENTS LATER –   CUT TO:

                    DAVID
               (to camera)
          It's very simple. This is my last campaign stop. In
          the next month, my opponents will spend an estimated
          combined total of 178 million dollars campaigning for
          your vote. I, too, will spend 178 million dollars. On
          you. If elected, I will send each and every registered
          voter a check for 4,072 dollars and 65 cents.

David holds up a GIANT CHECK to "Joe Public."

DAVID (CONT'D)
So, the only question for you America, is, "How are you going to spend your 4,072 dollars?"

David points at the camera and grins. We hear applause and the WINNER BELL goes off. Everyone is stunned.

ON TV: CLOSING MUSIC AND THE CREDITS OF THE DEBATE

CUT TO:

INT. SPORT 'N LOUNGE

In a cruddy hometown bar, the usual bunch of blue-collar types are watching the debate.

GUY ONE
I'm voting for that fella, what's his name?

OLD DRUNK
Clat Dross.

GUY TWO
Three cheers for Clat Dross!

They all do one big cheer.

ALL
Clat Dross! Clat Dross! Clat Dross!

As they cheer we pan down their greasy faces, ending on a very sad, quiet fellow on the end who explodes...

BOB
His name is David Cross!

But no one hears him over their cheering.

CUT TO:

INT. RADIO STUDIO

Bob as the radio talk show guy from before, TOM RITE.

                    TOM
              (irate)
          It's crass! It's blatant! This guy's trying to buy your
          votes, folks, that's it! That's all it is! And I for one
          am thrilled! Because this guy, this "David" is buying
          my vote from me! Not paying off some mega-conglomerate!
          He's paying me! And I like it, he's got it, and I'm right!

Again, in one swift motion he cues his theme music, drops his headphones
and plays a video game.

                                                            CUT TO:

EXT. SAME STREET FROM BEFORE

We see the SAME POSTER as before.

                    REPORTER (O.S.)
          What are *you* going to do with your money?

                    MAN ONE
              (excited)
          I'm gonna get me one of them all-in-one massage chairs
          with a built-in stereo in the ear parts!

                                                            CUT TO:

                    WOMAN
          I'd like to finally take that dream vacation to Reno...
          or Las Vegas, whichever one has better odds.

                                                            CUT TO:

                    MAN TWO
          Hello big-screen TV!

                                                            CUT TO:

                    GROUP OF COLLEGE GUYS
              (screaming into camera)
          MONEY!!!

                                                            CUT TO:

MUSIC SWELLS AS WE WATCH DAVID GETTING ELECTED...

As we watch an ELECTION DAY MONTAGE of all the people we just saw coming out of polling places and cheering—they just made four thousand bucks! David is acting very dignified in his voting booth until just after he votes, then he BURSTS from the booth, jumping up and down, pumping his fist and screaming in other VOTERS' faces.

DISSOLVE TO:

EXT. PODIUM

David's presidential INAUGURATION. Thousands of people are there. CHANCE and two EXECUTIVES flank David. David is finishing the oath. A white-haired JUDGE reads the oath. David is very excited, looking around, waving to famous people.

                    JUDGE
          ...and do you swear to uphold the Constitution?

                    DAVID
          ...to uphold the Constitution.

                    JUDGE
          And follow the will of the people.

                    DAVID
          ...follow the people.

                    JUDGE
          And lead...

                    DAVID
          ...lead.

                    JUDGE
          ...to the best of my ability...

                    DAVID
          ...ability...

                    JUDGE
          ...in the eyes of God.

                    DAVID
          Yeah, yeah, yeah...

                    JUDGE
          You may now be the president.

Fanfare plays. David shouts.

                    DAVID
          Let's kick some ass!

Big cheers and hugs all around. Chance and Mr. Hartnut grin and shake
hands. Hartnut hands Chance a large briefcase.

                    DAVID (CONT'D)
          Thank you.

On a stage off to the side is an R&B GROUP. It's comprised of THREE BLACK
SINGERS and ONE WHITE SINGER. They are dressed in flowing silk pajamas,
gold chains, etc.

                    DAVID (CONT'D)
          Now ladies and gentlemen, please welcome, with the
          inaugural song, Sir Groove-alot Records recording
          artist from Pennsylvania: Funkadelphia.

                    SINGERS
          Ooooohhhhh...
               (speaking)
          Oh, baby, you've been around over two hundred years but
          you still lookin' good to me. What'd you say your name
          was? America? Damn, baby, I'm gonna make love to you for
          four years.
               (singing)
          With the finest champay-ay-ayne...

The song continues. From out of nowhere Chow-Chow rolls up to David.

                    CHOW
          Uncle! Uncle!

                    DAVID
          Hey kiddo, how's it going?

                    CHOW
          Uncle! You're the president! Now you can get me my
          special shoes for my fat feet.

                    DAVID
               (chuckles)
          Now that I'm president there's a lot of things I intend
          to do. I'm going to get a satellite dish and watch
          whatever show I want, whenever I want. I'm gonna crank-
          call people...

                    CHOW
          Oh. And special shoes, Uncle? Special shoes for me?

                    DAVID
          I'm not finished! I'm gonna party all day, take a party
          nap, and then party all night with the best, most
          partyingist international celebrities that'll make you
          wish you'd never been born.

David is approached on both sides by CHET, a young executive, Mr. Hartnut,
and Chance. He shoves Chow away.

                    CHET
          David. Uh, Mr. President, congratulations.

                    CHANCE
          Well, this is it, we done it. You take care 'n' do what
          Mr. H says.

Mr. Hartnut steps up, smiling ear to ear. David looks at him with a mix of
obedience and uncertainty.

                    CHANCE (CONT'D)
          Enjoy this now. Like my Uncle Flip said: you're on the
          tip-top of the mip-mop.

This registers with David, where has he heard this before?

MUSIC: Sad-ish melody.

                                                              CUT TO:

EXT. BUS DEPOT.

Bob walking through a decaying, industrial part of town. He passes several holes in the ground.

> BOB (V.O.)
> Dear David. Hey, long time no hear from you. Ha ha. Well, I'm back home. Nothing much has changed. My old high school...

Bob passes a high school with the sign: "Vice President Humphrey High: Courage in the Face of Certain Failure."

> BOB (V.O.)
> ...the old plant...

Bob stands before the gates of a smoke-spewing factory with the words "Stacking Plant, a Division of Globo-Chem" on a sign.

> BOB (V.O.)
> ...my parents' house...

Bob is on a street of identical suburban homes, he's knocking on one door.

> BOB
> Come on, Dad, open up!

Bob pounds on the door. A NEIGHBOR answers. He is not happy. Bob realizes he's missed his parents' house by one house, and apologizes.

> BOB (CONT'D)
> They're all still here.

INT. CLASSROOM

Bob sits in a classroom chair, listening intently.

> BOB (V.O.)
> I got a job performing, so, I'm keeping the dream alive.

ANGLE ON: the TEACHER, TRILL!

> TRILL
> It ain't brain surgery. If you do well, you'll get to play America's favorite corporate spokes-thing—you'll

get to wear the blue-head! Pit Pat! And share his joy
with children! Who wants in?

The class all applaud, too excitedly, and TRILL slams them hard with his
tough-guy act.

> TRILL:
> All right, kiddos, this class is not for the weak. You're
> all my bitches now, and you have to EARN that costume—

ANGLE ON: Pit Pat costume hanging on a display—Bob is in school to play a
Pit Pat mascot.

> TRILL (CONT'D)
> ...and it don't come cheap. Open your Shakespeare to
> page thirty-four and begin reciting....

DISSOLVE TO:

INT. MODERN STYLE L.A. HOME - NIGHT

We see the Hollywood sign through a picture window and hear a TOUR
GUIDE'S spiel.

> TOUR GUIDE (O.C.)
> Keeping a promise he made during his campaign, the prez
> built this new White House in Hollywood, allowing him to
> remain closer to the people and the stars we all love.

Reveal Interior, L.A. White House.

MUSIC UP: Background, rap

Lots of couches, a big TV, Italia 2000 furniture, Nagel prints, track
lighting. Amongst this crap are some traditional paintings of past
presidents. The TOUR GUIDE is leading a group of MIDDLE-AGED TOURIST
TYPES.

> TOUR GUIDE
> The new White House has over thirty-seven television
> sets. One is over your head right now.

They look up to see a big-screen TV over their heads, playing *Reservoir
Dogs*.

> TOUR GUIDE (CONT'D)
> There are over twenty-four beers on tap, including the
> prez's own microbrew. He has his own casino, a drive-in
> closet, and air-conditioned shoes.

> VISITOR
> Where does he get his work done?

> TOUR GUIDE
> Good question. This is the signing room.

She crosses to a door with the words "Signing Room" on it.

> TOUR GUIDE (CONT'D)
> And if we're all real quiet, we can watch him at work.

She opens the door. The tiny room is a hubbub of activity, with David at
a desk in the middle of it all. David is signing papers with Globo-Chem
executive, Chet, looking over his shoulder. He notices the tourists.

> DAVID
> Hi, Donna! Hey, everybody!

Tourists smile and wave.

> DAVID (CONT'D)
> Hey, you guys be sure to check me out on TV. I'm gonna
> be in an episode of *Hooter and Pooch*, and I'm hosting
> *Amazing Exploding Animals* on . . .

Chet shoos the tourists away and closes the door.

> DAVID (CONT'D)
> Wait, I was talking to them, they're my fans.

> CHET
> No pool party until you finish your signing.

David pouts.

> CHET (CONT'D)
> I'm serious.

David signs. We follow a DOCUMENT as it is put on a stack. A MAIL CART comes by, picks up the stack. The cart is labeled, "New Laws."

CUT TO:

INT. SPORT 'N LOUNGE BAR

Back to Bob's hometown bar. The REGULARS are here, smiling and opening their giant prop-sized CHECKS from the government.

> OLD DRUNK
> Bartender, 4,072 dollars' worth of beer, please.

Everyone laughs as the BARTENDER serves the drunk. Bob is sitting in a booth. He has the Pit Pat costume on with the big blue head resting on the table next to him. Bob's DAD enters.

> DAD
> What the hell are you doing with that thing?

> BOB
> Oh, this is just temporary until David gets me a Hollywood acting job. It's called the Coattail Theory, Dad.

> DAD
> He ain't gonna give you no job. Nobody never gave nobody else anything, ever.

> BOB
> (trying to do the math)
> So, that means . . . everybody gives everybody everything all the time!

Dad scowls at Bob and then tosses an envelope at him.

> DAD
> This letter came for you today.

> BOB
> Hey, it's from David! See, this is it!

Bob opens it.

CLOSE ON THE LETTER

FLAT VOICE (V.O.)
"Dear Citizen, we got your letter. Enclosed is a picture
of the president with Willie Nelson. Yours Truly, the
World's Best Government."
(with a TM stamp)

Bob sets the letter down, sad.

CUT TO:

INT. STACKING PLANT LUNCHROOM

There is a makeshift dais, set up at one end of the room. The PLANT
MANAGER stands up at a podium with Bob's Dad. The Manager reads from a
card. Only about a third of the seats at the dais are occupied. Round
lunchroom tables fill the rest of the room. People are eating their
lunches only half paying attention. A BANNER hangs up behind the dais. It
reads "Congratulations On You're (sic) Retirement, And/Or Birthday!"

PLANT MANAGER
Anthony Odernklik, you have been working at this plant
for forty-two years, today you are retiring. Please
accept this chocolate watch as a token of our esteem.
May it keep track of the sweet time that lies ahead of
you when you eat it.

Applause as Bob's Dad stands up at the dais.

DAD
Thanks, Mandy. As I look out at this collection of
peoples, I see my boy. His name is Bob. Bob, I have a
surprise for you. I've arranged for you to take over
my workstation counting boxes. Also I have purchased a
burial plot for you on top of mine, so you can follow
me. Well, I guess my work here is done. I'm gonna go now.

With that, Bob's Dad clutches his heart and immediately collapses to the
floor...The Plant Manager looks at the chocolate watch and checks the
dad's pulse.

PLANT MANAGER
He's dead.
(to Bob)
You start next week.

The Plant Manager takes a bite of the chocolate watch. Bob is sad.

                                                    DISSOLVE TO:

EXT. MODERN SCIENCE LAB

This is the Walsh Institute. A sign in the foreground reads:

"The Walsh Institute. Where the present and the future meet. And make love."

                        DR. WALSH (V.O.)
            Gentlemen, ma'am, welcome to the Walsh Institute.

                                                    CUT TO:

INT. MODERN SCIENCE LAB

Mr. Hartnut, Chet, Todd, Ron, and Jane are being led by DR. WALSH, a scientist, through some labs. The first is typical, with a SCIENTIST looking through a microscope.

                        DR. WALSH
            As you can see, in this lab we're doing biospectral
            viral research, developing colorful new diseases...now
            step this way.

In the next lab, a SCIENTIST oversees FIVE SEVEN-YEAR-OLD CHILD LABORERS who sit on the floor, toiling away.

                        DR. WALSH (CONT'D)
            We're nearing the edge of the cutting edge of sneaker
            technology. If you'll step through here...

They enter another lab where a PATIENT is having his face operated on by TWO DOCTORS in surgical scrubs. A HUMAN FACE floats in a jar next to him.

                        DR. WALSH (CONT'D)
            This is nothing, just doing a routine face switching.
            But in here...

Dr. Walsh flashes a security badge to an ARMED GUARD who opens a "Top Security" door. The group enters a pristine lab. On one wall is a curtain.

>   DR. WALSH (CONT'D)
>   ...is what Mr. Hartnut has been dreaming of for years.
>   Prepare to be amazed.

Dr. Walsh opens the curtain, revealing a glass display area. In the display a small four-dimensional globe floats in the air about eye level. The globe looks like a mini-Earth, with green and blue areas. But it's somehow a bit different. Amazed reactions from the EXECUTIVES.

>   DR. WALSH (CONT'D)
>   What you see before you is a miniature planet. It has
>   its own atmosphere. It supports life...And it was built
>   in this laboratory.

CLOSE on HARTNUT'S face reflected in the glass.

>   MR. HARTNUT
>   Gentlemen, Glen Meadow Estates will be the first,
>   private, planned, gated planet. One-third the size of
>   Earth.

>   CHET
>   What's it made of?

>   DR. WALSH
>   The infrastructure is a metal gridwork, but the primary
>   material, the bulk of it, is dirt.

>   ROD
>   Dirt? From where?

Dr. Walsh uses a diagram.

>   DR. WALSH
>   Earth. Pure Earth dirt. Or simply, "earth." We've been
>   stockpiling for some time, digging holes and hollowing
>   in a wide circle. Everything remains fine on the
>   surface. It's a process called "undermining."

The Execs react with amazement, awe, some concern; this is a big deal.

>   DR. WALSH (CONT'D)
>   It weakens the earth's crust, but it's for a good cause.

                    RON
Holy frack.

                    HARTNUT
Glen Meadow Estates will have a controlled climate,
private security, a 3,019-hole golf course, the real
Lake Tahoe, the real Eiffel Tower, real Niagara Falls,
all within thirty miles of each other. All the best, for
those who can afford it.

                    JANE
          (realizing)
A better world for better people.

Everyone is in awe. A BEAT, then...Mr. Hartnut accidentally cuts a small
fart.

                    MR. HARTNUT
I'm sorry, I'm just very proud.

                                                        CUT TO:

EXT. HOLE - ANYWHERE

A large industrial tube is sucking up dirt out of a small hole. We hear a
whistle.

                    FOREMAN
          Okay, that's all we're getting out of this one. Haul her
          out!

We hear the familiar "beeps" of a truck backing up. It is loaded with dirt
and pulls away from the hole. On its side is a Globo-Chem logo. Another
crew swoops in behind the truck and puts up security tape and metal
barriers like we saw in Branson.

                                                        CUT TO:

EXT. L.A. WHITE HOUSE POOL

David and COREY FELDMAN sip Bloody Marys poolside. David wears a terry-
cloth robe, Corey has his trademark sunglasses and black fedora.

                    DAVID
        So Corey, you got a part for the prez in *Car Wash
        Academy II*?

                    COREY
        Oh, bro, I got you hooked up.

                    DAVID
        All right.

                    COREY
        Hey, you talkin' to "the Feldman," beeyatch.

A BUTLER enters with papers.

                    BUTLER
        The morning papers, sir.

Corey takes *The Hollywood Reporter*, David takes *Dramalogue*. The cover
has a picture of David on it, with the headline, "The Prez's Improv
Background."

                    DAVID
        Got to keep up on the news.

                    BUTLER
        And sir? Here are your scripts for tomorrow's press
        conference. I've had the big words spelled out
        phonetically.

                                                        CUT TO:

EXT. SHITTY MALL

Establishing.

INT. SHITTY MALL - BATHROOM

Sounds of shoppers and muzak. Bob is dressed to perform in the Pit Pat
mascot costume. He looks in the mirror, adjusts the head. It's "showtime."
He walks out the door.

SHITTY MALL FOOD COURT

SFX: Cheesy music

Bob as Pit Pat, dances around on a raised platform in the center of the MALL. No one pays attention. A sign by the stage reads: "A visit from Sergeant Manners from 1:00 to 2:00 - 2:00 to 3:00 Pit Pat - 3:00 to 4:00 The Button Doctor."

                                                              CUT TO:

INT. GLOBO-CHEM MEETING ROOM

Todd, Jane, and Ron are working. A bank of TV monitors has the news on it. Jane draws everyone's attention to a news report.

                          JANE
              Hey, shhh. Everybody, you should see this.

A female ANCHORETTE, SUSAN, reads the news. She sits at a National News Desk. The graphic in the upper third reads: "More Cave-Ins."

                          SUSAN
              Good evening. A poverty leak in India threatens
              millions, and in the Midwest more unexplained cave-ins
              leave thirty-two people homeless. Here with that story
              is Pompeyo Duarte.

                                                              CUT TO:

TV NEWS REPORT

EXT. BY A COLLAPSED HOME IN A HOLE

A very ethnic-looking reporter, POMPEYO (DAVID), speaks. He does not speak English very well and struggles with the language throughout.

                          POMPEYO
              Yes, okay, I stand at a hole which...fall open. Eh, eh,
              two o'clock in afternoon. Many people hurt, surprised,
              frightened. You see emergency people working can you.

ANGLE ON: Emergency crew helping distraught people.

                          POMPEYO (CONT'D)
              It very tragic, sad, sad. Susan?

>   SUSAN

Pompeyo?

>   POMPEYO

Yes?

>   SUSAN

These mysterious collapses seem to be occurring with
greater frequency, with the causes still unknown. Do you
have any idea what might have caused this particular
one?

>   POMPEYO

Yes, yes, yes, okay, yes.

BEAT.

>   SUSAN

Yes, you do?

>   POMPEYO

Yes, there has been others.

>   SUSAN

Right, but what might be the source?

>   POMPEYO

I'm sorry...sauce...

>   SUSAN

Oh.
>   (to camera)
It seems like we're having technical difficulties with
our audio, we'll rejoin Pompeyo...

>   POMPEYO

No! No technical difficulties. I hear you fine. But this
word, this "sauce," saorse, I don't know...

INT. GLOBO-CHEM MEETING ROOM

The Execs watching this report on TV are concerned.

INT. WHITE HOUSE

Yet another party in progress. David, in a loose jogging suit and sunglasses, sits with giddy PORN STARS and PAULY SHORE.

>   DAVID
>   Hey, you douches want any more sushi?

They all do. FOUR CHINESE DIPLOMATS enter, accompanied by a Chinese INTERPRETER.

>   INTERPRETER
>   Mr. President, The Trade Leader of China wish to offer
>   their respects.

>   DAVID
>   It's all good.

>   INTERPRETER
>   This is Minister Chong Li Quang...

>   DAVID
>   Cool, cool...Ah so, Mr. Chong. This is Tisha St. Rue,
>   Selena Lacroix, Beef Thomson, Brittany Lee, Jaqui Oasis,
>   and Pauly Shore.

>   QUANG
>   (Chinese)

>   INTERPRETER
>   Minister Quang says, "You will see, Chinese prisoners
>   will make superior golf equipment."

David just stares at him, then David and the Porn Stars and Pauly Shore all laugh—

>   DAVID
>   That shit's hilarious. Talk like that again!

An AIDE runs up to David, handing him a script.

>   AIDE
>   Mr. President, sir. There's been an emergency, you have
>   to go on television and read this.

                                                  CUT TO:

INT. OVAL OFFICE

It is lit for a broadcast. Someone is applying the finishing touches to David's makeup.

> FLOOR DIRECTOR (O.S.)
> On in...5...4...3...2...

> DAVID
> My fellow Americans, hi. It's me David, I'm the president. It is with the deepest of hearts that I regretfully inform you that at 6:14 Eastern Standard Time, the state of Indiana collapsed and caved in, causing untold injuries, fatalities, and horrific loss of property. Firstly, I would like to reassure the citizens of the United States that the Indiana Pacers, the Colts, and all professional and collegiate sports teams will continue to play their schedules. We don't know the cause of this tragedy, but the FBI and the CIA are doing things. I can't go into it because...

David nods in an off-camera direction, suggesting that there's somebody in the room that he can't talk in front of.

> DAVID (CONT'D)
> But rest assured, American Pride Goodie Bags are being flown in, and will be distributed. Thank you, may God continue to bless America, and now, more TV.

CUT TO:

INT. GLOBO-CHEM MEETING ROOM

Scientist Walsh is holding some soil in his hand, pours it into a container. The EXECUTIVES burst in.

> TODD
> Dr. Walsh, these cave-ins are getting worse.

> JANE
> Can't we put something in the holes, to fill it in?

              DR. WALSH
   Yes, yes. The best thing I can devise is this foam. It
   hardens, and can support as much weight as dirt.

              TODD
   Oh. Great.

They seem relieved. Then...

              RON
   Why don't we just build our new planet out of that foam?

              DR. WALSH
   Well, it's poisonous.

No reaction.

              RON
   Also it costs more than dirt.

              ALL
   Ahhhh.

BEAT.

              RON
   What's the main ingredient?

              DR. WALSH
   Poison foam.

Execs nod. We PAN across the room and out the window. Hartnut is in the
courtyard again, wearing the Pit Pat outfit, thinking.

                                  CUT TO:

EXT. OUTER SPACE

Earth is floating beautifully in the distance. The Space Shuttle enters
the picture and slows to a halt. We hear the conversation of the shuttle
crew.

              SHUTTLE CAPTAIN (V.O.)
   Shuttle Two in position.

> COMMAND CENTER (V.O.)
Unload cargo.

Shuttle doors open and a large, somewhat loose, pile of dirt floats out.

Camera pans as the dirt drifts over to "land" amongst other dirt that is collecting, somehow, on a gigantic metal frame floating in space, being welded as we speak by lots of floating astronaut welders.

EXT. OBSERVATORY

SUPER GRAPHIC: "FjslKrank Observatory, Finland"

INT. OBSERVATORY

TWO serious FINNISH SCIENTISTS take turns peering through the telescope and exchange excited Finnish reactions...which are SUBTITLED.

> FINNISH SCIENTIST #1
Jogel! Come quick! This is freakin' my ass out!

> FINNISH SCIENTIST #2
Aye Carumba!

INT. SENATE FLOOR

We see the Senate floor filled with Congressmen. A MALE and FEMALE NEWS ANCHOR are blue-screened over the scene.

> MALE ANCHOR
Good evening. Tonight is the first State of the Union address of President David's first term.

> FEMALE ANCHOR
A tumultuous first one hundred days.

> MALE ANCHOR
Yes. One filled with controversial new ideas: moving the White House, selling public lands, three new holidays, including Fox News Day.

> FEMALE ANCHOR
He's been busy. And he promises some surprises tonight.

MALE ANCHOR
Yes, a press release promised that at some point he
would transform the Constitution. We'll see what that
means.

FEMALE ANCHOR
I believe he's about to enter.

Audio of Senate chamber.

The lights go out and are replaced by swinging spotlights.

SFX: Space Age Sounds.

The Announcer's Voice changes to that of a BASKETBALL ANNOUNCER.

BASKETBALL ANNOUNCER (V.O.)
Ladies and Gentlemen, please welcome, your President of
the United States, David!

MUSIC: Gary Glitter's "Rock n' Roll Pt. 2" plays in the room

David enters, high-fiving reluctant SENATORS all the way up the aisle.
David arrives at the podium.

MUSIC: Changes to ethereal magic special music

David begins setting up a Chinese box.

DAVID
(shouting over the music)
Ladies and gentlemen. Citizens! For years the mysteries
of the Orient have been precious and few. One such
mystery is the mystery of the vanishing peacock. Known
for its amazing plumes, it's almost impossibly beautiful.

David opens a side of the box and reveals a beautiful PEACOCK.

MUSIC: Sting

DAVID (CONT'D)
But as amazing as a peacock may be to see, they are even
more amazing to see...disappear.

In a flurry of motion, David shuts the box, drapes a cloth over it, taps it, and the box collapses. David pulls the cloth up, revealing nothing!

MUSIC: Crescendoes

There is silence from the congressmen. The lights return to normal. David, unfazed by the lack of reaction, begins his speech.

> DAVID (CONT'D)
> Thanks, I've been really getting into magic. All right, all right. Wha's up, D.C.?

David holds for a response that doesn't come.

> DAVID (CONT'D)
> All right, psyched to be here. For my next trick I need a volunteer. Is there a pretty senator from Colorado in the hizzouse? Come on, what do ya say? Dianne?

Congressman are humfering and fumfering, not sounding pleased.

> CONGRESSMEN
> Boo!

> DAVID
> Come on, who's brave? Let's get some encouragement going for a volunteer.

The boos become louder as more people join in.

> DAVID (CONT'D)
> (pointing)
> You sir, you look like a sport, huh?

ANGLE ON: OLD, STODGY POLITICIAN CUPS HIS HANDS AND YELLS OUT.

> POLITICIAN
> You suck!

The boos become deafening. People are yelling out all kinds of nasty things. David reacts over announcers.

> MALE ANCHOR (O.S.)
> Wow, I've never seen this.

>   FEMALE ANCHOR (O.S.)
>   They're really turning on him.
>
>   DAVID
>   (making the "pouty" fish face, as he is about to start
>   crying)
>   What's going on? I thought you liked me? You guys are
>   being real jerks.
>
>   MALE ANCHOR (O.S.)
>   The President is really getting emotional.

David starts to walk offstage. Pens and cups are thrown at him. His walk
quickly turns into a run.

>   FEMALE ANCHOR (O.S.)
>   And is he . . . yes, he is running away.
>
>   MALE ANCHOR (O.S.)
>   I've never seen Congress make a president cry before.

>   DISSOLVE TO:

INT. WHITE HOUSE - NEXT DAY

The party is over. David sits at his table, but the room is empty. Just
Corey Feldman and TWO PORN STARS, with TWO ROCK GUYS passed out. David is
distraught.

>   DAVID
>   Where is everybody? I should never have made that dumb
>   speech.
>
>   COREY
>   Hey man, you were great.
>
>   PORN STAR
>   Yeah.
>
>   DAVID
>   You think so?

Corey and the Porn Star agree.

                    PORN STAR
          People who heard the speech on the radio were completely
          fooled by that magic trick.

                    DAVID
          That's cool. You guys are my real friends...

Pauly Shore enters, wearing a bra, underwear, a long fur coat and throwing
glitter around.

                    PAULY SHORE
          Look at me! I'm living the high life! Life is good!
          Whooo!

Everybody claps, but stops when Pauly pulls out a GUN...similar vibe to
that great scene in *Boogie Nights*.

                    PAULY SHORE (CONT'D)
          Whoo! Play my song, bitch!

A KOREAN ASSISTANT presses play on a boombox and we hear The song "Sister
Christian" which Pauly dances to, as he yammers.

                    PAULY SHORE (CONT'D)
          This is it! I got the look, baby! Check out my
          coattails!

On this word, ANGLE ON DAVID and push in as Pauly keeps talking.

                    PAULY SHORE (CONT'D)
          I got the longest coattails ever made!
               (gunshot)
          Everybody can ride my coattails!
               (gunshot)
          Whoooo...I'm the coattail king!

Multiple gunshots and everyone in the room scatters, except for David,
who is frozen, his mind focused on...

                    DAVID
          ...the tip-top of the mip-mop...

A single tear rolls down David's cheek.

EXT. THE FAMILIAR GLOBO-CHEM GUARD GATE

Outside the Globo-Chem office building, Bob pulls up in his
rattletrap car.

                    GUARD
        ID?

Bob hands him the ID and talks.

                    BOB
        Bob Okendorf. I'm Pit Pat.

Bob gestures to the Pit Pat costume in his backseat.

                  BOB (CONT'D)
        I mean, I'm an *actor* who will be portraying *Pit Pat*
        today for the kids in the day care. I'm very honored to
        see the home of Pit...

The GUARD interrupts him. Couldn't care less.

                    GUARD
        Yeah, go on...whatever.

Bob drives on. Parks.

INT. GLOBO-CHEM HALLWAY

Bob is walking around with the bulky costume slung over one shoulder,
trying to follow directions from a piece of paper...

                    BOB
        ...okay, the day care...where is that? Oh, better get
        in my costume first.

Bob enters the EXECUTIVE MEN'S ROOM to change.

INT. MEN'S ROOM

VERY NICE men's room. Bob is in one of the PRIVATE TOILET STALLS,
changing.

                              BOB
          "Take it from me—I love you!" "Take it from me . . . Take
          it *from* me, *I* love *you!*" Oh, what is it Mr. Catalanano
          reminded me about? "Acting is the action and speech all
          balled together in a big glob." Something like that.

INT. GLOBO-CHEM HALLWAY

JANE, one of the Execs, is frantically searching for Mr. Hartnut, walking
down the hallway . . .

                              JANE
          Mr. Hartnut? They need you, sir . . . they need you in the
          research room!

She stops by the Executive Men's Room, not sure if she should enter it . . .
she finally pushes the door open a bit and calls in.

                           JANE (CONT'D)
          Mr. Hartnut—they want you, sir! Hello? Anybody?

Suddenly, a Pit Pat appears (it's Bob, but she thinks it's Hartnut
wandering around in one of his "thinking" interludes).

                           JANE (CONT'D)
          Oh, excellent. You're needed. Right away. Follow me.

INT. HALLWAY

Jane and Bob walk down another hallway.

                              JANE
          We've got an update on the new planet for you. Very
          important. You need to hear this.

Bob stops for a moment by a door that says, "Day Care Center." We can see
kids in the room, waiting to meet Pit Pat.

                           JANE (CONT'D)
          Not there. Sir, please, follow me!

Jane hustles Bob towards a black door at the end of the hallway with the
words "Security Clearance Required" on it.

                         JANE (CONT'D)
          Right, here, sir, let me get this for us...

Jane punches in a code, breathes into a tube, and spits onto a flat black
square on the security label.

                    FEMALE COMPUTER VOICE
          Identiscan complete. Please enter Jane Tasselbock.

Jane smiles at Pit Pat (Bob), as they walk through the security door
into...

INT. GLOBO-CHEM MEETING ROOM

In the room we've seen before, the same group of young executives are
gathered around the table, along with the scientist, Walsh. Throughout
this scene we occasionally view it through Bob's POV, inside the mask.

                         EXECUTIVES
          Hello, sir. Hello Mr. Hartnut.

Bob stands there, unsure of what to do, does a little Pit Pat wave. The
Execs aren't sure how to respond to this...they carry on.

                         TODD
          Sir, everything is on schedule.

                         JANE
          The planet should be ready to move into shortly.

Slide of a beautiful green-and-blue planet.

                         RON
          The dome is almost in place and the golf courses will be
          ready for play on Friday.

Slide of ELDERLY COUPLE in leisure wear, smiling and playing golf.

                         TODD
          And sir, we've practically sold every plot on the planet.

                         RON
          All your friends, sir, they've all bought houses.

                    TODD
          The richest people on Earth.

                    JANE
          The cream of the elite.

                    CHET
          The rich and creamy people.

                    TODD
          But...um...

They all look to Walsh.

                    WALSH
          Uhhh...There is one small matter. It seems that in
          building the planet, certain biological instabilities
          have led to the metamorphing of insects, well, one
          insect...uh...
               (spilling the beans)
          There's a giant ant on the planet.

                    CHET
          But it's still just an ant.

                    JANE
          It won't eat much.

                    WALSH
          Well...

                    CHET
          More important is the matter of the planet's core and
          energy source.

Slide of a drawing of a planet's inner workings. Its infrastructure is
comprised of beams, wires, and pipes, with a nuclear symbol in the core.

                    WALSH
          Yes, the mass of plutonium needs carbon-based organic
          matter before it can set off its perpetual reaction.

                    JANE
          A body.

> WALSH
> Preferably a human being.

> TODD
> Just one.

> RON
> We wanted to suggest someone. It all ties together so neatly.

> JANE
> You're going to love this.

> CHET
> We thought this—what if, after he appears at the opening ceremonies, we lower the President himself into the core?

Slide of smiling David.

> JANE
> He'll die, of course, but who better?

> CHET
> We couldn't have done it without him.

> RON
> The little rapscallion.

> TODD
> So, that's it. Any questions, sir?

A panicked BOB just stands there. Then he waves.

> TODD (CONT'D)
> Sir?

> BOB
> Take it from me, I love you.

Bob starts backing away, waving, nervously feeling for the door handle behind him. He gets a hand on it and leaves.

> EXECUTIVES
> Bye, sir.

Bob is gone. The Executives breathe a sigh of relief. They look around at each other.

>   RON
>   Whew. Good job.

>   CHET
>   Yeah. Who made these graphics?

>   TODD
>   I did. On my own PC.

>   CHET
>   Get outta here.

>   JANE
>   You mean you made moving 3D images with four-color
>   graphics and six-point optics on a portable PC?

Todd pulls out a disc.

>   TODD
>   Yeah, it's all with Quantel 87 software.

>   CHET
>   Quantel, huh?

>   RON
>   That's bad.

>   TODD
>   It's superbad.

>   RON
>   Can I borrow that?

>   TODD
>   I'm sorry, my brother, but you're gonna have to get your
>   own.

Their attention is diverted by the door opening up. Pit Pat walks through.

>   JANE
>   Yes, sir?

                    TODD
         Did you have any questions?

The real Hartnut removes his Pit Pat head, revealing his own sweaty,
greasy, unhealthy pallor.

                    HARTNUT
         I'm late, I was having a tinkle. So, let's get going
         here, I want to hear everything.

                    RON
         Uh...sir?

                    HARTNUT
         Let's go, give me the update.

                    RON
         Heh. Nice one.

                    HARTNUT
         What the fuck are you giggling about, you retard? I told
         you I was tinkling.

The EXECS are stunned.

                    HARTNUT (CONT'D)
         Fine! I was dropping a deuce, you got me. Now what's so
         goddamned urgent?

The Executives all look at each other, worried. They realize they told the
secret plan to a Pit Pat.

                    JANE
         Uh...we fucked up.

INT. GLOBO-CHEM HALLWAY-MOMENTS LATER

Hartnut, still in the costume, but with the head left behind, walks in
a quick stride down the hallway, trailed by his young execs...he is
barking out orders.

                    HARTNUT
         Tell the crews to keep digging—we're not slowing down,
         that planet WILL open for business ON TIME. Get me the
         biggest ant spray bottle we have—get me twenty of 'em.

Warm up my escape pod—*always* keep my escape pod warm. Tell the President that he is being invited on a secret trip to the moon—we'll use him to ignite the plutonium core. Got it?

                    JANE
          Yes, sir, right away!

                    HARTNUT
          And one more thing.

He stops in his tracks.

                    HARTNUT (CONT'D)
          Kill all the Pit Pats.

SFX: DRAMATIC MUSIC: STING

MUSIC UNDER FOLLOWING MONTAGE: A CHORAL PIECE SUNG IN LATIN PLAYS THROUGHOUT.

This montage is an homage to the murder sequence from *The Godfather*.

                                                        CUT TO:

EXT. HIGHWAY - EVENING

Bob in the Pit Pat suit is driving his shitty car, fast, we know not where. He removes the Pit Pat head and mutters—

                    BOB
          Got to warn David.

                                                        CUT TO:

EXT. ARIZONA SHOPPING MALL

A PIT PAT is waving to kids and saying, "I Love You." A black car pulls up, TWO GUYS get out and spray him with bullets from a machine gun.

                                                        CUT TO:

INT. WHITE HOUSE - NIGHT

David is being chased by someone down a never-ending hallway...this is a dream. We cannot see the chasing person's face, only hear his laughter.

David falls, the CHASER descends on him with a screwdriver. We finally see his CHASER'S face—it's DINO!

INT. WHITE HOUSE - NIGHT

David wakes up, crying his patented baby cry. He looks over to see the PORN STAR sharing his bed. She looks at him funny, like you would look at an adult man who cried like a baby. He sheepishly gets out of bed. He is wearing a long nightgown.

                                                              CUT TO:

INT. "JONNY SPAGHETTI'S" ITALIAN RESTAURANT - CONNECTICUT

A PIT PAT is sitting at this family restaurant eating a big plate of spaghetti with the CHIEF OF POLICE across from him. The WAITER, a sinister-looking TEENAGER with a big fake cardboard moustache, approaches the table. The waiter pulls a sawed-off shotgun out of nowhere and shoots the Pit Pat and then the Police Chief, who slumps into his plate of spaghetti.

                                                              CUT TO:

INT. WHITE HOUSE HALLWAY

David wears a long nightgown and stocking cap. He smiles weakly at the menacing SECRET SERVICE AGENT who stands guard outside his bedroom door, and walks down the hall.

                                                              CUT TO:

EXT. ENTRANCEWAY - OFFICE BUILDING - IDAHO

A PIT PAT is about to enter a revolving door, as two GOONS are watching. He pushes the door halfway and the GOONS shove a crowbar under the door, wedging it. He is confused. They shoot the Pit Pat, spraying blood all over the window.

                                                              CUT TO:

INT. WHITE HOUSE KITCHEN

Still sweating from his nightmare, David pours himself a glass of water. He is trying to formulate a plan, glancing around, paranoid. We can hear party noises in another room.

CHARLIE SHEEN enters, laughing, with a PORN STAR (Tisha St. Rue) on one arm.

> CHARLIE
> Oh, hey man.

> DAVID
>> (scared)
> Huh?

> CHARLIE
> It's me, Charlie. Are you all right?

> DAVID
> Yeah, I'm fine. Bad dream.

> CHARLIE
> Oh. Hey, whose house is this?

> DAVID
> It's mine. What are you doing here?

> CHARLIE
> Partying...right?

> DAVID
> Yeah, no, I mean yeah. Ha ha. It's a party, have fun.

> CHARLIE
> Cool, come on, Debbie.

Charlie and the Porn Star turn to exit.

> DAVID
> Wait, you just called her Debbie. Her name is Tisha
> St. Rue.

> DEBBIE
>> (laughs)
> That's my stage name. My real name's Debbie.

> DAVID
> What?! No...NOOOOOOOOOO!

Charlie and the Porn Star exit, laughing. David is devastated by this news, even more scared than before, trying to think.

                    DAVID (CONT'D)
         Overton was right!!! I've got to warn Bob!

                                                    CUT TO:

INT. WHITE HOUSE

David is frantic. He starts testing doors to find an exit. The first one
opens to a ransacked billiard room with a ROCK BAND crashed out in it.
A silent SECRET SERVICE AGENT is watching the group, he looks sternly at
David. David grins at him, shuts the door, opens another, nothing. Then a
third door, and finds . . .

INT. WINE PANTRY

David is very frightened now.

                      DAVID
         Shit! Supplies, I'll need supplies.

He grabs a bottle of wine and puts it in his shirt. Grabs another, same
thing, and another, but this time when he pulls the bottle the whole rack
pulls open, it's a false door opening into . . .

INT. LAB

Like the lab in JAMES BOND films, but there is only one thing in it, a
strange-looking car.

                                                    CUT TO:

INT. MASSAGE ROOM

A PIT PAT is getting massaged (with costume on). There is a ruckus by the
door when A GOON enters. The Pit Pat reaches for some giant oversized
glasses (that would fit over the costume) and puts them on. He is shot
through the lens (a la Moe Greene in *The Godfather*).

                                                    CUT TO:

EXT. HIGHWAY - NIGHT

Bob is still driving. He looks in his rearview mirror and notices a black
van following him.

                         BOB
          They're following me . . . shoot!
          Got to try to throw them off . . .

Bob notices a DINER on the roadside. He turns in to the parking lot,
squealing his tires as he does so.

                                                        CUT TO:

INT. DINER - NIGHT

A PIT PAT (with Bob's distinct Pit Pat head) is at the counter. He has a
plate of half-eaten eggs and a cup of coffee in front of him. TWO GOONS
enter and gun him down from behind. Blood sprays everywhere. The GOONS
exit. The costume keels over, the head rolls off—there's NO ONE INSIDE.
Busted ketchup bottles fall to the floor. Bob, now wearing only underwear,
has been watching from his car and freaks out: he'd propped the Pit
Pat suit at the counter as a decoy, but he never suspected it would be
"murdered"! He peels into reverse and out the parking lot.

EXT. HIGHWAY - NIGHT

Bob is auxiously driving, wearing only underwear. He pulls into THE NEW
White House valet lot and gets out.

                         BOB
              Finally!

Other PARTYING CELEBS are picking up their cars. They, too, are in their
underwear—so Bob doesn't stick out that much. He tosses his keys to the
valet and enters.

MUSIC: End of montage music

                                                        CUT TO:

INT. WHITE HOUSE BASEMENT

David is frantically writing a note. He finishes, takes a sip of water from
his glass, then notices "H_2O" on the gas cap of the car. He opens the cap,
pours his glass of water in, and the car magically, immediately starts up.

                         DAVID
              Weird.

He gets behind the wheel.

David sits in the car, presses a button, and a hidden garage door opens, revealing BOB in his underwear in a dramatic pose.

>   DAVID (CONT'D)
>   Hey! You look like Bob!

>   BOB
>   David!

>   DAVID
>   Yeah. I look like David!

INT. SAME - MOMENTS LATER

Bob and David stand beside the car, which is still running.

>   BOB
>   What's going on? Is this your car?

>   DAVID
>   It is now. It's water powered. I was trying to kill myself.

>   BOB
>   Kill yourself? With steam?

David nods and hands Bob the letter he had in his pocket.

>   BOB (CONT'D)
>   (reading)
>   "To anyone who cares, I'm sorry everyone hates me. I was
>   only trying to be good. I guess I tried too hard."

>   DISSOLVE TO:

CLOSE-UP OF LETTER

It is written in a young girl's hand, with drawings of big eyes crying, and sad childish illustrations.

>   BOB
>   "Sometimes people are really insensitive, they look at
>   me and see an ugly caterpillar that scares them because

I am 'gross.' But they don't stop to see the fragile
unicorn made of glass that lies underneath." David, this
is deeply embarrassing.

                    DAVID
I know. Bob, I've got to tell you something that's gonna
blow your mind!

                    BOB
I know, man, I know already. I found out by accident.
I had no idea of the extent of it. Look, you shouldn't
blame yourself.

                    DAVID
I don't. I was suckered in, like everyone.

                    BOB
Yeah, we all were. What are we gonna do about it?

                    DAVID
What *can* we do? Boycott the porn industry?

                    BOB
Well, I guess that's a start, but . . .

                    DAVID
But then we're just punishing ourselves! Dammit! Tisha
Lynn, Mercedes St. Whatever, why?

                    BOB
Wait, I think that we stumbled across two different
horrible conspiracies. Look, let's both say them at the
same time, just to be fair.

                    DAVID
Right.

Bob and David look each other in the eyes, take a breath, and
simultaneously launch into their explanations . . .

    BOB   DAVID
The earth is being stolen from   Porn stars have fake names.
under our feet to build a private
planet for rich people.

A pause. They both gasp, and shudder.

>   BOB
>   Wait, did you hear what I just said?

David thinks, then...

>   DAVID
>   Earth's being stolen...private planet...rich
>   people...our feet...
>   (gasp)
>   That's terrible! Hey, how come you're not wearing any
>   clothes?

>   BOB
>   (shrugs)
>   Ah, you know.

>   DAVID
>   Oh my God, it's all my fault. What's the plan now?

>   BOB
>   Listen, the core of that new planet is unstable
>   plutonium. If we can just get down in there with an
>   explosive we can blow that thing to smithereens.

>   DAVID
>   Done.

They shake hands emphatically—

>   BOB
>   Of course we'll die.

David withdraws his hand.

>   DAVID
>   Hm.

>   BOB
>   But we'll save the Earth.

>   DAVID
>   Yeah, but—

>
>   BOB
> Don't forget, you caused it to happen.

>   DAVID
> I know, but still, not dying would be preferable.

>   BOB
> But we wouldn't really die. Not in a historical way!
> We'll be heroes, and someday two guys who look a little
> like us would do monologues onstage as us. And people
> would cheer and we'd live forever.

>   DAVID
> No, I get that. Our look-alikes wouldn't be dead, but we
> would be. Probably forever.

>   BOB
> Yes. I see your point.

They mull on this for a moment, then:

>   BOB (CONT'D)
> Unless . . .

>   DAVID
> Unless what?

>   BOB
> I've got a plan! How fast does this water-powered car go?

>   DAVID
> How fast do you want it to go?

>   BOB
> Nine thousand miles an hour.

>   DAVID
> It goes three hundred.

>   BOB
> Why didn't you just say that?

>   DAVID
> I thought you'd say you wanted to go, like, ninety . . .
> then I'd impress you.

                    BOB
Good try. Do you have any guns?

                    DAVID
No!
        (beat)
Oh wait, no, I have hundreds.

                    BOB
Get them. I'll drive.

                                              CUT TO:

EXT. HIGHWAY

From a superwide shot, we watch the water-powered car driving superfast
down this lonesome stretch of highway as the sun comes up. The car comes
to a stop. Out of water.

                    BOB
Shoot. Out of water.

                                              CUT TO:

EXT. HIGHWAY

Bob and David are both peeing in the gas tank. In an "homage" to
Zoolander, they start having a "sword fight" and slo-mo peeing all over
each other as they giggle.

                                              CUT TO:

Back to the car as it peels off down the highway.

EXT. GUARD GATE

The water-powered car bursts through the guard gate into the Globo-Chem
parking lot.

INT. GLOBO-CHEM ATRIUM

CORPORATE EXECS are milling about, coming in for their morning.

Bob and David burst in, waving guns around.

                    DAVID
Ladies and gentlemen, I don't mean to harm ya, don't
mean to alarm ya, I just mean to charm ya! This is not a
holdup or a foldup.

                    BOB
Globo-Chem has committed illegal acts against the people
of the world. We are here to expose hypocrisy, destroy
the monopoly, and do it properly!

David looks at Bob—

                    DAVID
Good rhyme.

Bob looks at David—

                    BOB
I thought of it a few years ago. I'm just happy to have
found a use for it.

They look out to see they are surrounded by dozens of GLOBO-CHEM SECURITY
with guns drawn.

                                                    CUT TO:

INT. GLOBO-CHEM MEETING ROOM

Bob and David are tied up. Guards are standing around. Hartnut enters.

                    HARTNUT
David Cross . . . Bob Oden-whatever . . . What were you
thinking?

                    BOB
Can we say something, sir?

                    HARTNUT
What?

                    BOB
We weren't thinking.

                        DAVID
Give us another chance. Let us come in a different way.
Through the air-conditioning ducts.

                        HARTNUT
Not today, boys, not today...

                        DAVID
Well tomorrow's no good for me.

                        HARTNUT
Shut up.

Hartnut opens a window hatch in the ceiling. He looks up at the night sky.
Hartnut plows through the following monologue, ignoring Bob and David's
asides.

                        HARTNUT (CONT'D)
The stars are beautiful at night, aren't they?

                        BOB
Okay.

                        HARTNUT
They say that for every person with a dream, there's a
star.

                        DAVID
I'm sorry, where are you getting your statistics from?

                        HARTNUT
Then, of course, you have your black holes.

                        DAVID
I'm not gettin' this down.

                        HARTNUT
Antimatter, emptiness, a drain on the universe.

                        BOB
Kinda like this speech.

                        HARTNUT
It's interesting...

                    DAVID
          Not like this speech.

                    HARTNUT
          Black holes...

Bob and David groan.

                    HARTNUT (CONT'D)
          ...are more powerful than stars. In fact, they swallow
          stars. Well, that's what I am, boys, I'm a black hole,
          and I am hungry.

                    BOB
          I get it.

Hartnut picks up a RED TELEPHONE under a cake plate.

                    HARTNUT
                (on telephone)
          Get me the blue telephone.

An EXEC walks in with a blue telephone under a different cake plate.
Hartnut picks it up.

                    HARTNUT (CONT'D)
                (on telephone)
          Operation Green Meadow is Go. Implement Phase One!

Claxons ring and red lights spin.

Chet, Jane, Todd, and Ron run into the room and strap themselves into
chairs. The DATA SCREEN shows the exterior of the office building.
Hartnut straps himself into a chair in front of the Data Screen. This
office set now resembles the bridge of the Starship *Enterprise*.

                                                        CUT TO:

EXT. GLOBO-CHEM BUILDING

The office building transforms into a rocket, taking off.

SFX: Jet engines roar to life.

CUTAWAY to an amazed Bob and David—childlike wonder.

EXT. ROCKET SHIP

The side of the rocket reads (in cursive writing like the name on the back of a boat): "My Kid's Inheritance." It enters the stratosphere.

CUT TO:

INT. CONFERENCE ROOM/BRIDGE OF ROCKET

Turbulence shakes the room as everyone watches the liftoff on the BIG SCREEN.

> HARTNUT
> To the Tippity-Top of the Mippity-Mop!

> BOB
> Hey, that's our saying.

> DAVID
> Well, we didn't say the "ippity" part.

> BOB
> Still.

> DAVID
> But if we're going to be honest about—

> HARTNUT
> Shut up! We need to listen to this. Stupid FAA regulations.

Bob and David and the Young Execs all watch an informational video on the big screen before them.

> NARRATOR
> Hello, and welcome to the McDonnell Douglas S-5 office building, interstellar aircraft.

A cartoon diagram of the office building. Cheap animation of the building's facade falling away and rocket taking flight.

> NARRATOR (CONT'D)
> Developed in association with NASA as an office building
> slash rocket ship, the S-5 is both an office building
> and a high-powered space travel device. So sit back,
> relax, and get back to the grind.

On the screen we see the Globo Planet fast approaching. It is a green
planet inside a bubble. As we get closer we can make out golf courses,
nice suburban homes and a mountain range and an ocean, and one GIANT ANT.

> HARTNUT
> (to Bob and David)
> Jealous much?

CUT TO:

EXT. PLANET SURFACE

A small CROWD OF RICH-LOOKING WHITE PEOPLE, including Chance, are
gathered where the ship has touched down. It is the end of a tiny main
street, similar to Branson's, but cleaner, very artificial. There are no
cars, only golf carts.

The rocket door opens and Hartnut, wearing a high-collared robe, exits
the ship to APPLAUSE. In the distance is the Earth, strikingly large. A
HYPERACTIVE EMPLOYEE overdoes the cheering.

> EMPLOYEE
> Three cheers for Mr. Hartnut!

> CROWD
> Hooray!

> HARTNUT
> Thank you. Well, we did it. We built ourselves a better
> world for better people. I see Carlyle and Bunny
> Richmond, who built their fortune with zero money down.

A typical MIDDLE-AGED COUPLE from a late-night "make your fortune"
infomercial.

> HARTNUT (CONT'D)
> Jarred Spoon...

A RICH YOUNG MAN, smoking a cigar, smiles at Hartnut.

> HARTNUT (CONT'D)
> ...you did it. With nothing but the sweat of immigrant labor. Charles Keating, thank you for being here. James, Rita, Carlowe, you are all loaded, God bless you. Now, to begin. Dr. Walsh?

Dr. Walsh stands off to the side on the edge of a hole. Bob and David are tied up and dangle over the hole from the end of a crane.

> DR. WALSH
> Yes. Soon you will be able to take off your weight belts. By lowering this sampling of organic carbon matter into the plutonium core we will achieve a reaction necessary to provide full, Earth-like, gravitational pull.

> HARTNUT
> And look who's providing us with the necessary raw materials. It's our good friend, the President of the United States, and his dancing partner.

Applause. David can't help but smile and wave.

> DAVID
> All right, people! Are you ready to party?!!

> HARTNUT
> Well, you gentlemen don't seem too upset about transforming into globules of antimatter.

> DAVID
> No, man, we're into it. Let's do this, we love it.

> BOB
> Yeah, did we give you the impression we didn't want to organically implode? Geez, no.

> HARTNUT
> Very well, then. Here to do the honors is my great-grandchild, Elsinore.

We see a really cute LITTLE GIRL, about six years old.

                              ELSINORE
                    The children of the world are our future.

Everyone applauds the little girl and they toast each other and chatter
happily.

                                 BOB
                    Oh, geez, I'm not listening to this crap.

                                DAVID
                    Yeah. Children ain't shit, and I'm sick of hearing it.

Hartnut is peeved.

                               HARTNUT
                    Why are you ruining this perfect day?

                                DAVID
                    Look, can I say a few words for the adults in the room?

                                 BOB
                    Hey, assholes!

Everyone shuts up and listens.

                                DAVID
                    Listen, folks, we should be totally honest with you. Bob
                    and I are gonna be famous.

                               HARTNUT
                         (laughing)
                    Oh yeah, how's that?

                                DAVID
                    We're gonna blow up this planet, and then be on the
                    news. Bob?

David looks over at Bob, who is slumped over, motionless. Is he dead...?

                            DAVID (CONT'D)
                    Bob?

                                                              CUT TO:

EXT. BRANSON STREET

Bob and David in their show clothes (Bob in suit, David in shorts and T-shirt) are sitting on the steps of their favorite bar, both are operating puppetronic remote devices like the ones DINO used to manipulate the mechanical bears earlier in the movie. Both wear thick glasses that allow them to see what their doppelganger robots on the future planet are seeing.

> DAVID
> . . .Bob—wake up!

> BOB
> This thing is jammed.

REVEAL Dino, the puppeteer, sitting next to Bob, he reaches over and flicks a switch on Bob's remote control and we

CUT TO:

EXT. PLANET SURFACE

The BOB ANIMATRON comes back to life!

> BOB
> There we go—here I am again. Whew, sorry. . .I conked
> out for a second there. Where were we again?

> DAVID
> I was just explaining about how we're going to blow up.

> BOB
> Good. Yes. Let's do it!

The Mechanical Bob and David open up their chests to reveal scary thermonuclear BOMBS. The assembled rich people gasp and step back.

The Bob and David Animatrons reach into their mechanical chests and hook wires together, adjusting calibrations.

> HARTNUT
> What the hell? You're not people. . .you're some kind of
> robots.

                    BOB
The best kind of robot—the hero kind!

                    DAVID
One second, almost hooked up.

                    HARTNUT
What the hell is going on?

                    BOB
Let me explain. Here's the deal, there are six different
kinds of stars in the sky...I think.

                    DAVID
Yeah, and then there are black holes. Now, black holes
suck.

                    HARTNUT
I know, I know, I'm the one that told you about that
shit.

                    BOB
Right. Okay, well then, we're all set. I guess there's
nothing left to do but...

ANIMATRONIC Bob and David press the buttons on their chests
simultaneously and—

                                                    CUT TO:

EXT. MAIN STREET - BRANSON

View of the new planet in the night sky - BLOWING UP

ANGLE: The humanoid Bob, David, and all the actors from town are gathered
on the front steps of their favorite bar, looking up, watching the
explosion.

Bob and David remove their simulation eyeglasses and enjoy the giant
explosion along with their actor friends. People applaud.

                    BOB
          It's beautiful, isn't it?

> DAVID
> Wow. Yeah, it's a shame so many rich people had to die.

> BOB
> Hey, that's the first time in history that's ever been said.

CHOW-CHOW rolls up.

> CHOW
> Uncle, Uncle!

> DAVID
> Hey, little big guy.

> CHOW
> Ha ha, Uncle, you're so funny, I'm sad.

> DAVID
> Oh, why?

> CHOW
> Doctor said 'cause I didn't get my special shoes my feet are gonna swell up and choke me to death.

> DAVID
> Oh.

Bob is looking really sad. To David he motions . . .

> BOB
> We gotta go.

> DAVID
> Listen, Chow. I hear you. I'm gonna do everything in my power to help me gain more power so I can gain more power. See, I want to have so much money that I can buy all the special shoes in the world, and just . . . burn 'em. Just 'cause I have that much money. And there's nothing you can do to stop me.

They share a moment. Behind David, Bob pulls up in a HOT RED SPORTS CAR. He has THREE LARGE-BREASTED WOMEN in bikinis in the back seat.

                    BOB
          Hey David, you ready?

David nods to Bob.

                    DAVID
          Oh, yeah.

David pats Chow on the head, jumps in the car. Bob hands David some Ray-
Bans. They both put a pair on.

As Bob and David strike poses, we hear the outro song "Cool Summer"—
a typical '80s teen movie theme a la *Footloose*. They high-five. FREEZE
FRAME. Over the following song we see the CREDITS and STILLS of Bob and
David posing with volleyballs, big-titted girls, cool cars, and in various
scenes that just plain weren't in the movie. In every scene they have '80s
clothes and haircuts.

Bob fighting with a GUY IN A HAWAIIAN SHIRT.

David in a lifeguard chair with a gorilla peeking out behind him.

Bob and David in all-black clothes at night, sneaking by a sign that
reads, "Ridgemont All-Girl Academy."

Bob and David mooning a graduation ceremony.

The very last picture, before the song fades out, is Man One sitting in
his massage chair.

                    SONG
          Cool Summer / We're gonna have a cool summer! / We're
          gonna play volleyball in the sand / And rock 'n' roll
          with a rock 'n' roll band / Cool summer gonna be all
          right / We're gonna sleep all day and sleep all night! /
          We're gonna beat up some strangers who live out in the
          sticks / and find some chicks to suck our dicks! / Pull
          some pranks, rob some banks / Take crystal meth and
          snort some crank! / Cool Summer! Yeah!

FADE OUT.

"Studio Notes" on "Hooray for America!"

From: CASEY Voldemortz, Production Head, ********* pictures

To: Everydamnbody at this studio

Re: Hooray for America! screenplay

Are we making this thing?! I was at my summer-summer home in Amagansett (I rent the same place every year, it's three houses down from my summer home and right between LaBarbara's and LaLorne's, but keep that under your hat), ready to relax, read a few scripts, see and be-seen, and make some GD deals when I looked up to find this turd-in-waiting script awaiting me. I called G.T. my V.P. at three A.M. and he said it wasn't green-lit yet, but was aquamarine, verging on green, and so I put aside sleep for another day and dug in. Here are my thoughts:

Who are Bob and David? Do we care? Can this be Brendan Fraser and Pauly Shore? If we can't get Fraser, what if Pauly plays both parts? Wait, what am I talking about? "If we can't get Fraser"?! Of course we can. Scratch that. THE ONLY THING I UNEQUIVOCALLY LIKE is this serio-comic "promotional" section that opens the film (pp. 135–36) But please FIND OUT: Are these real products? Wonderful opportunity for Product placement! SOMEONE Call Marketing. Don't we make rabbits? Get Karyn on this.

RE: THE CHARACTER OF CHOW-CHOW (p.139) This is a wonderful opportunity for INTERNATIONAL SALES!! But can we find a cute Korean kid who speaks English, for fuck's sake! The way this is written is borderline racist! Also kid doesn't have to be Korean, no? Jap, China kid, Filipino is fine, right? Or Hawaiian? Maybe Eskimo?

RE: CASTING (p. 141) Can we get Alec Baldwin for Mr. Hartnut? Probably cheap. His career is over. I just saw him on the beach doing his morning run – he has a stomach like a barrel of gefilte, wobbling to and fro.

I DO NOT like the political aspects - NO ONE IS INTERESTED IN SATIRE!!! (p. 142) But, should we make one of the candidates black? Thinking "24" or "Armageddon" here.

RE: THE MENTION OF CRAWFISH (p. 145) Note to my ASSISTANT, JENNY - "Crawfish" reminds me, Jenny, I'm having lunch at the Ivy with Bewkes, right? Find out if they have the smoked trout today, if not cancel lunch. Say I'm with SALMAN RUSHDIE – who, by the way, I just saw taking his morning constitutional on the beach. He was SHITTING IN THE OCEAN!! Good for him – I'd give anything to take a real dump.

RE: LOCATION (p. 146) Branson? Sounds expensive. Is this a real place? Can't we just shoot in the fucking Valley? Seriously. Don't be stupid.

RE: RATINGS!! (p. 146) I see a ref to "Brief Nudity"?? Who? One of these guys? Absolutely not! Let's get Jessica Alba in for this part? Or maybe what's-her-face? Yeah, let's get her.

RE: PLOT POINT (p. 146 thru 150) This whole song/tribute thing to "America". I don't get it. It's not funny. It MAY BE EDUCATIONAL, but NO ONE CARES!! People don't go to movies to LEARN ANYTHING! They go to movies to give money to people like me. Period. ALSO, is rapping still popular? Jenny, can you go to security and ask a black?

RE: MECHANICAL BEAR (p. 153) Can we get John Goodman for the Bear? He could do a voice-over or we could put

Goodman in Bear makeup. This thing needs some marquee names. Anybody!

RE: MORE MARKETING TIE-INS!! (p. 157) Regarding Pit Pat costume...possible tie-in? Can we make this a skateboarding "hoodie"? Who is PIT PAT? Will we get sued? Can we SUE SOMEONE ELSE IF WE MAKE THIS MOVIE? Look into it, that might be reason to give it a greenie!

- I stopped reading for a little bit. A lot of fucking talking in this thing. That's like, all it is. Do people like talking? Jenny, go outside and ask someone walking around.

RE: TV PARODY IN FILM (p. 163) Regarding junkie/reality show...possible spin-off? Having lunch with Burnett on Tuesday, will feel him out. Also, NOT going back to the Ivy! DeVito and Perlman hit me up for a threesome! No thank you. If it was Ron Perlman, then maybe. Rhea? ABSOLUTELY NOT!!!

RE: BRUNCH (p. 175) Am I still having brunch with Harvey and Anna on Sunday? Do I still drink? If I do let's make it at the Ivy. LOOOOVE their peach bellinis! I think. JENNY, Find out if I still like peach bellinis.

RE: LUNCH (p. 176) Jenny, where am I having lunch tomorrow? What's the name of the sushi place in the valley that Bay told me he got a handi from the hostess? Sushi Dushi or something like that? What was the name of the hostess? I'm guessing Lee or Kwan or something like that?

RE: SOMETHING IN THE SCRIPT (p. 183) I see a reference to an "el Presidente" Nice!! This is the fastest growing demographic in America. More of this! Maybe a Telenova tie-in?

OVERALL NOTES: I stopped reading at 184. It's 10 AM and time to MAKE SOME DEALS and GOUGE SOMEONE. I have to eat something and talk to someone – whose idea was it to vacation at a place so peaceful and quiet! I'm going fucking nuts! RE: THIS MOVIE - Jesus, I can't believe I made it through one-quarter of this turd on wheels. I would never see this thing. No explosions, no tits. Also no exploding tits. PASS!

BONUS SKETCH SCRIPTS!

GRAND RAPIDS' TOP NITE-CLUB
HAVANA NIGHTS CLUB and RESTAURANT and BATHROOMS
presents the comedy and musical stylings of the one and only

**LIMITED RUN!
24 MONTHS
ONLY!**

FAGIT & MORELLO

Full of Liquor-Lovin' Laffs and Scampi Savoring Songs!

Join the Gents in their latest Hijinks and Buffoonery Revue:
"SOUSED OF THE BORDER!"

MORELLO will sing his top-charting* song: "Sorta, Kinda, Maybe (in Love...or not)"
FAGIT promises to do all 12 versions of his 14 jokes and his 3 comic pantomimes.
He will move his arms and make faces!!

Featuring
The Vieja Girls!

ALSO APPEARING...

With 3 Showrooms available, it's Three-tertainment!!

In the **VEAL CUTLET ROOM:** Hand-Puppetry (with insults) by
MR. MUSTACHIO and **JIMINY JERKO,** his right-hand man!
In the **LIGHTFOOT ROOM: WILLIAM "THILLY BILLY" SWISHER**
and his **KICKLINE** - Girls, Girl, Girls, and One Boy...sort of!

HAVANA NIGHTS CLUB

Step Up To The Hi-Bar...
For the latest Special Drinks By
GORDY - Just out on parole!

CIGAR VODKA SMELTER- FISH AND FRESH CIGAR LEAF SWIRLED WITH VODKA
VEAL GIMLET - MADE WITH REAL VEAL
BANANA DAIQUIRI · EXOTIC FRUIT DRINK · BE CAREFUL!!!

*the song has been in the top 1000 for 3 months

FAGIT & MORELLO

by Bob Odenkirk and David Cross

Written in 2009

INT. BISHOP'S STUDY

A fat bishop in fancy dress sits behind a simple desk, speaking into a big microphone. This is ALL BLACK-AND-WHITE, sorta like newsreel, except for the film clips, which are like a black-and-white Martin and Lewis film.

                    BISHOP
          Hello fellow bishops, parish priests and devout
          followers, this is Bishop John McMurtry of the Greater
          Rochester Archdiocese, here to talk about a film that
          is coming to your community in this year of our lord,
          one thousand nine hundred and fifty-six. The film I am
          about to sample for you is wicked and venal. The images
          you are about to see are shameful and cause for great
          consternation, though the cinematography by Gerhard
          Deutsch is, as usual, nothing less than brilliant. The
          film features a newly discovered nightclub song and
          comedy team by the name of "Fagit and Montello," but do
          not be deceived by the lighthearted japery, this film is
          rife with blasphemy and scandal—

                                                        CUT TO:

EXT. DESERT FOOTAGE

Random Graphics fill the screen: "Laughingest!", "Singingest!", "Romancingest!"

                    ANNOUNCER (V.O.)
          Coming to the screen, laughs, songs, and more laughs!
          Get lost in the scorching desert with America's
          laughingest singingest new comedy-romancery team!
          "Fagit and Morello"! As they chase girls, and fortune,
          in the cradle of civilization! The Exotic Middle East!!

INT. DESERT STUDIO SET

Bob and David as a Martin and Lewis type of comic team. Bob is the Dean Martin (Morello), David is the Jerry Lewis (Fagit). They are in a fakey studio "Desert" set. Both have leather flying gear, like from the '40s, and speak in sorta dopey but lovable Brooklyn accents of the time.

            FAGIT
Hey you, Morello, where the heck are we?

            MORELLO
Hey you, Fagit, how should I know? You were the
navigator, you got us lost!

            FAGIT
Yeah, I'm sorry, now we'll never find the jade onyx of
King Kumutmutmut.

            MORELLO
Ah, shut up about that rotten stone. I need to find some
girls.

            FAGIT
You gonna put your cannoli in their spaghetti?

            MORELLO
You know it, chum. First, I'll sing to 'em, but there's
no way I'm singin' with this parched throat.

            FAGIT
Wish there was some water.

Along comes a COMICAL MERCHANT in a striped outfit selling water in
leather-bladder-type containers. Fagit grabs one and pours a bunch down
his throat and on his face.

            MERCHANT
No! You stop! Is holy! Holy water!

            MORELLO
Hey you, Fagit, stop it, that's holy water you're
drinkin'!

Fagit does a spit take.

            FAGIT
I thought it tasted kinda old.

            MORELLO
You know what that means? I guess we're in the Holy
Land.

Music starts and the Merchant and Fagit both become transfixed by Morello as he begins singing in a nondescript crooner style that is Andy Williams crossed with Bob Odenkirk...but more Bob Odenkirk.

                    MORELLO (CONT'D)
               (singing)
          Holy Land, Holy Moly land, Man Oh Man, This ain't no
          Charlie Chan...land—

The song cuts out as we

                                                        CUT TO:

EXT. FOOTAGE OF MIDEAST SITES

                    ANNOUNCER (V.O.)
          See the two knuckle-brains as they hunt for diamonds!
          Meet sirens and sahibs! And run into the holiest ghost
          of all, in *Fagit and Morello Meet the Ghost of Jesus!*

The TITLE: *FAGIT AND MORELLO MEET THE GHOST OF JESUS*

                                                        CUT TO:

INT. UNDERGROUND TOMB SET

The two guys, led by their SAHIB HELPER, a very white guy with too much tanning makeup on, walk around with flaming torches.

                    FAGIT
          Hey you, Morello, shine a light over here, I gotta pick
          my nose.

Morello shines the light at Fagit and he digs away in his nose with gusto.

                    FAGIT (CONT'D)
          Ah...sweet relief.

Behind Fagit is an illuminated tomb!

                    SAHIB
          Oh my goodness and gracious, it can't be!

> FAGIT
>
> What? Ain't you never seen nobody digging for nose gold before?

> MORELLO
>
> No, not that, Fagit. It's a tombstone. What does it say, Sahib?

> SAHIB
>
> It say, "This is the tomb of the one they call the Nazarene."

> FAGIT
>
> Haha! What kinda name is "Nazarene"?! That's a nutty name! They used to call my Uncle Morty the "Schnozzarene!"

Morello slaps Fagit.

> MORELLO
>
> Shut up, Faggoli, you're way off the mark! Don't you know who that is?

> FAGIT
>
> Naw, I don't, so who's it anyways?!

> MORELLO
>
> Christ!

> FAGIT
>
> Don't get mad at me, just tell me!

> MORELLO
>
> Jesus, you dope!

> FAGIT
>
> Christ Almighty, what are ya talkin' about?

> MORELLO
>
> That's it exactly!

> FAGIT
>
> What?

> MORELLO
>
> You got it!

> FAGIT
>
> I got what?

> MORELLO
>
> The one! He who am—that's who!

> FAGIT
>
> I've never been so confused! Jesus H. Christ on a cross!

> MORELLO
>
> Exactly!!

> FAGIT
>
> Why you!! Jumpin' Jesus! Answer the question! Whose tomb is it?

> MORELLO
>
> Well, I don't know if he jumped any, but he sure was a kooky kat!

Fagit has a fit, which ends as Morello sings in his trademark, white-bread warble...

> MORELLO (CONT'D)
> (singing)
> Jesus H, Whatshisface, the Leader of the human race—best guy ever, never mind the weather, he'll zap them clouds with his superpow'rs!

Cutting the song off again as we

                                                              CUT TO:

INT. TOMB

F&M are sitting on the lid of an opened grave, wiping sweat from their foreheads. Morello is asleep.

> FAGIT
>
> Ah, you go 'head an' sleep. I'll keep watch. There ain't nothin' in this tomb, anyways.

From behind Fagit comes the ghost of a very gentle-seeming Jesus.

> FAGIT (CONT'D)
> You feel a draft, Morello? Whew, all of the sudden it
> got kinda cold—

JESUS' GHOST puts his hand on Fagit's shoulder.

> FAGIT (CONT'D)
> Hey you, Morello! Is that...you? I-I-I thought you was
> asleep...I...

He turns around, gulps, his eyes pop at the sight of Jesus...

> FAGIT (CONT'D)
> M-M-M-Morello!

> MORELLO
> What is it, I'm tryna catch some winks!

> FAGIT
> J-J-J-Jesus!

> MORELLO
> God bless ya.

> FAGIT
> No...I mean the ghost of J-J-Jesus!

They both jump up and run.

INT. TOMB HALLWAY

Fagit and Morello run around, being chased by the ghost of Jesus as SPIKE
JONES "krazy" music plays.

Jesus throws some cream pies.

Fagit and Morello get stuck in a corner. Fagit accidentally pulls on a
gargoyle and they both fall down a hole.

INT. DIAMOND ROOM - LATER

We rejoin them now in a room with hieroglyphics on the walls. Fagit is being fanned by an UGLY FAT GIRL, and Morello sings his one hit song, "You Are the Moonbeam to My Starlight," to a HOT ARABIC WOMAN.

> ANNOUNCER (V.O.)
> And Morello sings his patented Top 70 hit—"Meatballs 'N Moonbeams!"

NOTE: Halfway through the song we see Jesus' Ghost casually hanging out.

> MORELLO
> (singing)
> For you are the moonbeam in my eyeball, the garlic calzone in my-a meatball, I wasn't nobody til you shone your light on me, Now I can see, that we, will be, in love...

The film "cuts off" suddenly, as if a projector was turned off, because it was, and we CUT TO the guy who turned it off—our BISHOP.

INT. BISHOP'S STUDY

> BISHOP
> That's enough of that. Now, when you see this film in your neighborhood you must get the entire parish out for a protest. Notify the radio and television. Get the word out! The more you protest, the more free publicity we can generate. Cinema Cattolica has produced these films for the express purpose of stirring up the rabble! If we can launch Fagit and Morello we already have a series of follow-ups being produced, including *Fagit and Morello meet Harriet Tubman*, and we have a script for *Fagit and Morello Meet the Harriet Tubman Robot*. Thank you, this is Bishop John McMurtry saying; "Let's find something to get peeved off about together."
> (he winks)

NINETEEN FIFTY-BLEVEN

by Bob Odenkirk, David Cross, and
Brian Posehn

Written sometime around 2003

Bob and David walk into a revival theatre. There is a newsreel playing, like an old-time newsreel from the '50s.

We pull in ON-SCREEN: A graphic for "Movietime News"

                    NARRATOR
          Movietime News presents, "The Year in Review"!

GRAPHIC: "The Year in Review—195*" (* signifies a symbol that is something between 4 and 5 but not an asterisk as it's used here.)

                    NARRATOR (CONT'D)
          Could this be the last decade featuring the year bleven?

CLOSE ON: A Calendar with the 1950-bleven symbol on it. A human hand reaches in and rips it down.

EXT. WHITE HOUSE ROSE GARDEN

THREE SCIENTISTS talk to a laughing PRESIDENT.

                    NARRATOR
          Scientists have asked the President to do away with
          the number bleven, the number between seven and eight,
          because they claim it screws up the deca-something
          system of counting. The President has agreed...

                                                          CUT TO:

EXT. SAME

The President signing an official order.

                    NARRATOR
          ...And has signed papers decreeing it so.

EXT. SAME

President speaks at podium.

                    PRESIDENT
          Everything that took place in this past year, or in any
          year ending with bleven, will heretofore be erased from
          the history books!

Assembled people clap halfheartedly.

                 PRESIDENT (CONT'D)
          The Army Corps of Engineers will assist all citizens in
          destroying any trace of this past year.

Applause.

ANGLE ON: A Jewish family outside a department store that has a sign that
says, "Wiltons—All are welcome! Jews, Blacks, Women, and Homosexuals
aren't welcome!"

                 JEWISH MOTHER
           (to camera)
          Oh well, it wasn't that great anyways.

EXT. SUBURBAN STREET, CIRCA 1950S

PEOPLE dropping off photos and papers from the past year in a Dumpster
labeled "BLEVEN THINGS." ARMY GUARDS stand by the Dumpster.

                 NARRATOR (V.O.)
          Good Americans everywhere respond to the call of duty,
          throwing away their photos, home movies, and diaries of
          the bleven year. Jimmy here is tossing away his prized
          4H Club medal for onion eating.

A KID proudly/sadly shows his 4H Club medal with the year "195-bleven" on
it. The ARMY GUARD salutes him.

                 NARRATOR
          Uncle Sam says "Thank you." Prisoners willingly go back
          to jail for one more year, happy to contribute. It's like
          they never served that time!

EXT. PRISON

Five BLACK MEN file in, getting cuffed by nasty GUARDS while a mean-
looking WARDEN, chewing straw and holding a rifle, looks on.

                        NARRATOR
          But this means that all achievements must be forgotten.
          Achievements in the field of science.

EXT. LAB

SCIENTIST speaks to camera.

                        SCIENTIST
          There were no significant achievements in science this
          past year to talk about. Just two and they're easily
          replaced. Something called "frogurt," which is a frozen
          yogurt no one will ever eat because it's disgusting. And
          this thing...

Holds up a test tube.

                        SCIENTIST (CONT'D)
          A cure for something called, "aidsies."

He tosses it into the garbage. Followed by a big sheaf of scientific papers.

EXT. SENATE BUILDING

                        NARRATOR (V.O.)
          Some events to be forgotten include one that most of
          America would *like* to forget. I'm speaking of Senator
          Howell Tankerbell's notorious blacklist.

INT. SENATE COMMITTEE ROOM

SENATOR TANKERBELL (a comically overstated Southern blowhard), sweating,
speaks to a panel of other SENATORS and many news microphones.

                        SENATOR TANKERBELL
          I have in this little book...

He holds up a little black book.

                        SENATOR TANKERBELL (CONT'D)
          ...A list of so-called Americans whom I suspect of
          being black.

Murmurs and brouhaha.

                    SENATOR TANKERBELL (CONT'D)
          Please, let me finish. The only way to truly find out if
          they are black is to ask them.

                                                        CUT TO:

INT. SENATE COMMITTEE ROOM

A sweating, nervous, BLACK WITNESS sits at the testifying table.

                    SENATOR TANKERBELL (O.C.)
          Answer the question! Are you now or have you ever been
          a black man in America?

                         BLACK WITNESS
                    (leaning into microphone)
          Yes.

The Gallery murmers as Tankerbell writes.

                    SENATOR TANKERBELL
          Thank you. Next!

We see a LONG LINE OF AFRICAN-AMERICANS waiting to step to the mic.

EXT. NYC STREET, MIDFIFTIES

                         NARRATOR
          And Madison Avenue will have to junk its efforts of the
          past twelve months and go back to the drawing board. Say
          good-bye to this fun product.

Cheesy kinescope commercial for "Li'l Cap'n" cigarettes.

A DAD sits reading the paper and smoking a cigarette. TIMMY, a ten-year-
old boy, enters and starts to take a cigarette from Dad's pack. The DAD
slaps his hand away.

                         DAD
          Hey there, son, those aren't for you.

                         TIMMY
          Aww, Dad.

                    DAD
Here.

He picks up a smaller packet of stubby cigs.

                    DAD (CONT'D)
Now kids have their own cigerettes. Li'l Cap'ns, they're
an inch shorter, perfect for your tiny, growing lungs.

                    TIMMY
Thanks, Pop.

They both light up, and Timmy takes a big drag.

INT. FAMILY ROOM

                    NARRATOR
And even entertainers are getting behind the enforced
amnesia...who can forget the Nutz Brothers and
their fabulous film *Knock Knock, Who's Scared?!* Well,
hopefully EVERYONE! Here's one last glimpse—

INT. HAUNTED MANSION HALLWAY

                    OFFSCREEN VOICE
Knock knock.

The NUTZ BROTHERS, THREE BROTHERS with identical suits and moustaches,
act scared and flop around.

                    NUTZ BROTHER 1
Whaaaa? Who's knocking?

                    NUTZ BROTHER 2
Answer it.

                    NUTZ BROTHER 1
I ain't answering it.

                    OFFSCREEN VOICE
Knock knock.

                    NUTZ BROTHER 1
Yeeeyeeee. What are we gonna do?

                         NUTZ BROTHER 2
          Let's answer it together.

                         NUTZ BROTHERS
          Who's there?

                         OFFSCREEN VOICE
          Mummy.

                         NUTZ BROTHERS
          Mummy who?

                         OFFSCREEN VOICE
          Your mummy, dummies.

They open the door to reveal an actor in a gorilla suit with an apron on,
who proceeds to hit both of them over the head with a rolling pin and
then shuts the door.

                         NARRATOR (V.O.)
               (chuckling)
          Truly the height of all things comedy. As well the war
          with Canada will also be forgotten.

                                                              CUT TO:

EXT. HUGE FIELD

In this field of well-mown grass is ONE WHITE GRAVESTONE with a soldier's
helmet hanging off it.

                         NARRATOR (V.O.)
          A war that lasted over eight hours and left one American
          infantryman's dog dead from Canadian measles, a gentle,
          mild form of measles similar to American measles but . . .
          not as good.

SCREEN SPLITS INTO FOUR featuring footage we've just seen.

MUSIC: RAH-RAH newsreel clap-trap theme

                         NARRATOR (V.O.)
          Nineteen fifty-bleven, seeya, sayanora, bye-bye,
          there'll never be another year quite like ya!

FAMOUS PUSSIES

by Bob Odenkirk and Brian Posehn

Written sometime around 2003

MONTAGE OF STILL IMAGES
Herbert Hoover, any President speaking to a group, Truman, Pearl
Harbor before it was bombed.

>ANNOUNCER
>Everybody talks about Roosevelt's "The only thing we
>have to fear is fear itself" line, but did you know that
>it was stolen from Herbert Hoover? Hoover, originally
>said, "The only thing we have is fear. Fear itself is
>the only thing we have. And you can take *that* to the
>bank!" And then Truman's "Have no fear, the buck stops
>here. I'm Superman!" speech, but does anybody remember
>Truman's first speech after Pearl Harbor?

INT. STATELY OFFICE

Black-and-white, scratchy newsreel (Super 8), crackly audio, Bob as
Truman.

>TRUMAN
>(a pronounced quiver in his voice)
>By now...you've all heard...what happened...
>(totally breaking down)
>Oh, my God...
>Holy shit...I am so fucking scared. I mean...oh,
>dammit...I'm scared. I don't want to die. I'm scared for
>me! I...can't stay here. No good...must...
>(yelling)
>—Warm up Air Force One!

>OS
>Uh...we don't have it yet.

>TRUMAN
>Well, somebody build one. Now!!

He runs off and we stay on the empty office...

>ANNOUNCER (V.O.)
>Or the so-called "great" President Kennedy's first
>response to the Cuban missile crisis...

INT. PRESIDENTIAL PRESS CONFERENCE

Wavy kinescope recording of presidential press conference.

> KENNEDY
> (heavy Kennedy accent)
> Aahhh...oh shit...aaaahhhh...I'm scared. My
> brother's scared. My entire family's scared. My wife. My
> girlfriend, we're all scared. And you should be, too.
> Arr, uh, I'm going to ask each and every American to
> stay home until I can get as far away as I can. Then you
> can, uhh, run, too. Don't panic. Wait until I am safe,
> and then it's every man for himself. (He shits himself.)
> Oh no. I sharted.

> CAMERAMAN (O.C.)
> There was no fart to that.

> KENNEDY
> (trembling)
> Ohhhh...

He sucks his thumb and cries. Over this:

> ANNOUNCER (V.O.)
> Cowardice has often been the first choice for so-called
> heroes all through time. Who could forget Lou Gehrig's
> famous speech.

EXT. BALLPARK

Black-and-white film, scratchy...David is Lou Gehrig...we catch a
snippet of the famous speech...

> DAVID
> Today I consider myself the luckiest man on Earth...

He carries on, we hear the voiceover.

> ANNOUNCER (V.O.)
> ...was preceded, before the game, by a speech with a
> much different tone...

EXT. BALLPARK

Same setting, David as Gehrig is a ball of self-pity and anger.

> DAVID
> Whyyy? Whyyyyy? I'm famous! I'm good at baseball!
> Whyyy?
>
> > (sobs—looking into the stands)
> I swear, I wish <u>you</u> had this! If I could rub a lamp and
> get a wish from a genie and give my disease to every one
> of you I would do it in a second! I would! I mean, come
> on, I'm probably better than every person here, you know
> that...

Cutaways to embarrassed PLAYERS and CROWD MEMBERS IN PERIOD DRESS.

> DAVID (CONT'D)
> I'm going to touch you...I don't know if it's catching,
> but I hope it is...

David as Lou Gehrig runs around, trying to touch the various BALLPLAYERS,
who scatter around the infield.

> ANNOUNCER (V.O.)
> The real first words, spoken before the moon walk,
> before the hatch opened, and we all heard the scripted
> "giant leap for mankind" thing, were much different
> before they went into a Hollywood studio and dubbed
> over them.

INT. SPACE CAPSULE

A futzy TV image, scrolling with snow, glitching in and out, relatively
stationary, of an ASTRONAUT (BRIAN POSEHN) with his hand on the door
handle, ready to exit. He is breathing heavy, and we hear the following
conversation with those famous "audio snow" blips in between talk.

> HOUSTON (O.C.)
> Are you ready to disembark?

> ASTRONAUT
> Uh, Houston...no, no, I'm not...

> HOUSTON (O.C.)
> Is there something wrong?

> ASTRONAUT
> Houston, yeah, it's wrong. We shouldn't be here! It's against . . . God! Whose idea was this?!

> HOUSTON (O.C.)
> This is Houston, could you repeat? Is there a problem?

> ASTRONAUT
> Yes there's a problem!! I'm fucking on the moon! Okay, I didn't know this till I got here, but I'm *scared of space*! I know it now! There's probably monsters out there!

> HOUSTON (O.C.)
> Uh . . . no, there's no monsters, over . . .

> ASTRONAUT
> (through the roof)
> You don't know! You're not here! I'm going home, now! MAKE THIS THING BRING ME HOME!!!

> HOUSTON (O.C.)
> Uh, this mission is not completed.

> ASTRONAUT
> It is now! I'm gonna scream in your ear until you bring me home! Ahhhhhhhhhhhhhh!

> HOUSTON
> Are you done?

> ASTRONAUT
> Are you bringin' me home?

No answer.

> ASTRONAUT (CONT'D)
> Aaaaahahhhhhhhhhhhh!!!!

Epilogue

Shortly after the fourth (and to some the last) season of *Mr. Show with Bob and David* finished airing, Bob was questioned by a confused fan at a gas station. "Hey, I thought you guys said you were doing another season? When's that gonna be on?"

Bob smiled ruefully and said, "We did and it was."

Our (perhaps only) fan had missed the whole stinkin' thing! The fourth season had already aired, quietly, secretly, in a dark corner of the cable channel known as HBO, or Home Box Office. A last-minute time slot shift from their vaunted "comedy block," where it followed *The Chris Rock Show*, to Mondays at midnight, where it followed *Taxicab Confessions*, made the fourth season a hidden gem—hidden even from fans who were LOOKING FOR IT. Painful. By the way, if you're wondering, that tank of gas cost Bob less than twelve cents, and he was able to drive over 4,200 miles on it (this was 1999).

Licking our wounds, we wrote *Hooray for America!* As we said in the Preface, it's not the first script in this book, but it is the first we wrote after the death of the TV show. Cinephiles and masturbators alike will note that the "Chow-Chow" character in this script also appears in *Run Ronnie Run*. "Chow-Chow" is directly inspired by our going to see the film *Rumble in the Bronx*…which you must see for the spectacle of a poorly dubbed and wheelchair-bound child (subbing for a legitimate English-speaking child) who will tug at your laugh-strings, as well as for the beautiful snowcapped mountains surrounding New York City (New York was busy with a bunch of rapes and murders that week, so Vancouver kindly subbed for NYC). Anyway, we invited the writers of *Mr. Show* to come in for a read-through of *Hooray!* Everyone thought it was funny but also agreed, immediately after reading, that the script couldn't be "our first movie" because it was too inside. And in addition it really required that the viewer be at least somewhat familiar with Bob and David, which, as we discovered from our gas-guzzling friend, was not anything to be counted on.

Thence came *Run Ronnie Run*. Yeesh.

The whole crew from the show wrote *Run Ronnie Run* as a "sketch" movie with an intentionally thin "road" story of the British producer taking Ronnie to Hollywood and interacting with a bunch of sketches. Over time, due to New Line's input and Bob Odenkirk's bad instincts, that story tried like hell to become more traditional. It failed on most counts.

We (and some of the cast) put together a live tour two and a half years later (2002), which was called *Hooray for America!* and utilized some aspects of that screenplay.

After all that, we knew we'd made a mistake drifting away from our strengths in sketch and so, despite a screaming lack of interest in our work, we wrote *The Bob and David Sketch Movie*, or *Bob and David Go to Hollywood*, or *Bob and David Make a Movie*, or *Six Months of Wasted Effort*—you pick your favorite title.

This would have been around 2003, according to the dates on the scripts.

In the very premise and title of *Bob and David Make a Movie* you can see our brains working on the issue consuming us: how do you get a movie made? More specifically, "How do WE get a movie made?" You are on your own. It felt like a surefire, home-run, steroid-spiked, laff-tastic hit. Hollywood disagreed. So thanks for reading our book! You're great. You're our fan? Fuck that, we're fans of YOU.

Acknowledgments

David would like to acknowledge global warming.

About the Coauthor

As Dictated to the Coauthor's Wife

Baby, what the fuck? Did you see this? My name's on the cover, yeah, but it's half the size of their names, and it's got a "with" before it, which . . . what the fuck? What? No, I'm not gonna call them! Fuck that. I mean, my picture's not even on the back. People know MY name, they don't even know BOB'S name, they just think he's "that guy." They still come up to me ALL THE TIME and say, "I loved you on Mr. Show with Bort and David*!" Bort's not even a real name! Huh? Yeah, turkey tacos are fine, but no cilantro on mine. What was I saying? Oh yeah, this book. No one's going to read it, it'll be like this year's* Brief History of Time, *people buy it just to look like they've got indie cred, but no one cracks the fucking spine even once. But the fucking picture . . . they didn't even tell me they were taking* *their fucking pictures! I know they said they'll give me my own picture, woman! You always fucking take their side! Yes, you do—why don't you marry Bob and David if you love them so much, see what kind of weird child they give you—bald little guy with shorts and an angry attitude! What? Are you crying? Honey... I'm, I'm sorry, I get worked up. You're the greatest. Come on... let me kiss you, come on... what are you writing? Everything I said? Everything? Well, let me see the picture of ME they are planning on using... huh... wow, I look like a real writer. Cool. Knowing them, they'll probably do something lame like stand near a dirty Hollywood sign. I'm being serious! Wait and see if they don't. Dicks.*